MARKET
SUPERMARKET
& HYPERMARKET
DESIGN

MARKET SUPERMARKET & HYPERMARKET

Edited by Martin M. Pegler

Retail Reporting Corporation, New York

Retail Reporting Corporation
101 Fifth Avenue
New York, NY 10003

Distributors to the trade in the United States and Canada
Van Nostrand Reinhold
115 Fifth Avenue
New York, NY 10003

Distributed outside of the United States and Canada
Hearst Books International
105 Madison Avenue
New York, NY 10016

Library of Congress Cataloging in Publication Data:
Main Entry under the title: Market Supermarket & Hypermarket Design

Printed and Bound in Hong Kong
ISBN 0-934590-33-8

Designed by Judy Shepard

Contents

Introduction

Supermarkets are a twentieth century phenomenon and as we are about to enter into the twenty-first century, we find that these markets are even more attuned to the changing times than many other retail outlets. They reflect who we are today — what we do today — and they even mirror our changing goals and aspirations. The supermarket is no longer an overgrown corner grocery — or just a place to buy provisions. In many cases, and especially with the Hypermarkets that are appearing in the U.S. — they have been firmly and successfully entrenched in Europe and Latin America for some time, — the supermarket has become a mini-mall, — an all-in-one shopping experience.

Today shopping is THEATER; there are lights for ambience, — lights for attention and lights for appraisal. There are lights to give signage a splash and a dash, — and lights to enhance the crisp greens of vegetables or give life to the sea-food, — or to make the hot and cold prepared salads seem more delectable. Designers are designing the supermarkets assisted by colorists, graphic artists and lighting specialists. These supermarkets are being created by Image-Makers — to project the right image for the targeted market which now include, besides the traditional home-bound mother, — the working mother, the father, the single dweller, those past fifty and still going strong as well as the teenagers.

Shoppers don't just buy brands anymore — they read labels. "Healthy Foods" are "in" and so are ethnic foods and foreign delicacies. Shoppers want choices — they want an in-depth selection; they want value for their money and though they may prefer a bargain — they will pay for what they really want. Like department stores, who they are beginning to resemble more and more, they need to keep the shopper in the store longer — to have them buy more. Now we are finding cafes, coffee bars and assorted fast food operations in Supermarkets. You can eat it and still buy more to take with you. Some are equipped with branches of banks so that you never need worry about running out of money, and there are VCR film rental shops and drug stores — all part of the supermarket design.

The Supermarket has become important enough to anchor a small mall or hold down a strip center. It's a place to meet — to see — to be seen — to eat — to attend demonstrations — hear lectures — learn about health — sample new taste sensations or rediscover old ones. Supermarket shopping is not drudgery — it can be fun and an adventure.

This volume contains a wide spectrum of food operations — from small, select and specialized markets — to convenience stores — to supermarkets — to the colossal, all-inclusive, Hypermarkets. Our selections cross this country and we reach into Europe, the Orient, Australia and Latin America for examples of how these markets are designed and how they are laid out. We have sought stores that have a "look" or "attitude" — that more than sell groceries, greenery, and canned goods, — they also "sell" a sense of specialness. We have tried to show the "Boutiquing" that is taking place in supermarkets; the specialization and in-depth presentation of products, and the appeal to the particular target market whether it be the Orientals who live and shop in southern California, — or the "health nuts" who frequent special supermarkets in northeast college towns, the Latino appeal in Texas and the sophisticated shoppers in Minneapolis and Los Angeles.

Rather than attempt to categorize the stores by what they are selling, we have grouped them by the amount of space they use to sell what they do. Thus, in the broadest sense — all our examples are Markets/Supermarkets/or Hypermarkets — and the difference is the space they need to develop their merchandise presentation. Some of our examples are actually parts of retail department stores, — others are parts of shopping complexes where you would never expect to find a food market. Our examples not only blend in, — they complement the retail stores around them.

To make some sense and put some order into the many strata of food stores, we have adapted the definitions specified by Progressive

Grocer magazine, generally considered to be the industry standard. We are indebted to the magazine and the editorial staff for the permission to reprint some of their material. We feel the terms are general and generic enough to provide at least a basis of understanding for the stores that follow in this book.

Food Store: Any retail store selling any variety of food, primarily for off-premises consumption. The specialty food store concentrates on one particular kind of food, like a fish store.

Grocery Store: Any food store selling a line of food and non-food items including canned and packaged products in addition to some perishable items. A grocery store is a food store and can be anything from a small, mom-and-pop corner deli, to a supermarket, or a convenience store.

A Convenience Store: Any compact, easy-access grocery store offering a limited line of high convenience items primarily for immediate use off-premises.

Supermarket: Any grocery store with at least $2 million or more annual sales that features self-service and a full line of groceries, non-foods, and perishables departments, including produce, meat and dairy. Because of the complex nature of what a Supermarket can be we have introduced them by type below.

- Conventional Supermarket: Any relatively undifferentiated, unadorned and standardized supermarket with middle-of-the-road pricing and selection. They are most frequently under 30,000 sq. ft. in size, carry about 12,000 items, provide service and may have some specialty departments.

- **Superstore:** A supermarket with at least 30,000 sq. ft. and a minimum (but usually well over) $8 million annual volume that offers an extended selection of non-foods along with very extensive service and perishables departments.

- **Combination Store:** Much the same as the superstore except that the percentage of space devoted to non-foods is at least 25%, and the store must have a pharmacy. The format evolved from the actual combination of

a drugstore and a supermarket being constructed side by side.

- **Warehouse Store:** A supermarket with more than 1500 items, primarily dry goods, with limited perishables departments including at least meat, produce and dairy, and low prices with low gross margin from reduced labor, service, selection and decor. A conventional supermarket that goes to discount pricing does not necessarily become a warehouse store.

- **Super Warehouse Store:** A warehouse store hybrid stressing price, as well as a wide selection of perishables and primary service departments such as deli and bakery. It is usually characterized by a minimum of 40,000 sq. ft. of total space, at least 15,000 items and over $15 million in annual sales.

Hypermarkets: An economy supermarket combined with a discount department store under one roof. This type of store requires a minimum size of 60,000 sq. ft. but is usually over 100,000 sq. ft. in space and carries an inventory of more than 30,000 items. This is originally a European format and Hypermarkets have been opening up in the United States (see last chapter). It is the largest and most capital intensive of all the Supermarkets.

In addition, we are pleased to present throughout this book design statements and philosophies by some of today's leading architects/ designers of supermarkets and hypermarkets. In their own words they explain what is involved in designing a successful selling space, — how merchandising, fixturing, lighting, graphics and signage — and the right colors can and do affect the creation of a special store, — make it inviting and also memorable. They explain that it is more than apportioning space and locating adjacencies, — it is more than laying in miles of fluorescent tubes and picking fixtures from manufacturers' catalogs. They are in the business of creating settings — moods and ambiences that sell.

We can't supply the smells of freshly baked breads and cookies, — of roasted coffee and exotic herbs and spices, but we hope our pictures will delight and stimulate all your senses.

Martin M. Pegler

Chapter One

Up To
20,000
Square Feet

F.L. Roberts

WESTFIELD, MA

Design: Architectonics, Huntington Station, NY

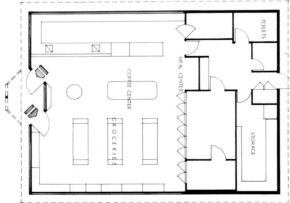

Dinesh Doshi, President of Architectonics
Jacob George, Sr. Designer
Rene Cruz, Jr. Designer
Richard Santoni, V.P. of Operations for F.L. Roberts
Doane & Williams, Cabinet work

The client wished to have his market position reinforced while, in the 800 sq. ft. space, they also wanted to create a sense of quality and service. In addition to fine tuning the merchandise plan, presentation was given equal importance with the emphasis on layout, fixturing, lighting and signage. The challenge to the designers was to encourage circulation throughout the store while exposing impulse items in the forefront at all possible opportunities.

The design strategy consisted of directing incoming traffic through a separate entrance door that would deliver the customer to the right side of the store, — circulating counter-clockwise to the service counter. From the custom designed coffee center, sight lines are open to the meal center and the cooler beyond. The gondola height was restricted to four feet to allow unobstructed views to the perimeter walls which are also low.

Varied light sources serve the store to make it appear warm and inviting. Natural light filters in from three exposures, and fluorescent tubes housed in ribbed chrome rails, are used to highlight the gondolas located beneath them. Tiny low voltage pendants emphasize the streamlined good-looks and efficiency of the coffee center which is the focal point in the store's total design. Neon signing moves from the exterior of the store through the interior and ties the store name up in a bright yellow band. To add to the excitement, — aqua sign banners hang down from a yellow suspended grid.

Simple Simon

HACKENSACK, NJ

Design: Architectonics, Huntington Station, NY

Using a palette of cool grays and a warm peach provided the designers with a subtle yet strong statement that separated this 2800 sq. ft. convenience store from the usual convenience store. In addition, by using patterned ceramic tile flooring and European-style deli cases, they also conveyed a message of quality to their up-scaled audience. The basic objective was to get the "convenience-oriented" shopper to shop the entire store with its diverse range of merchandise categories. A diagonal layout was strategic to the solution. By eliminating a right or left side only shopping pattern, the departments tended to overlap and flow one into the other.

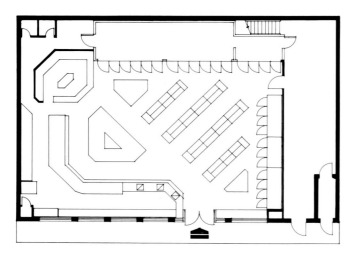

Dinesh Doshi, President of Architectonics
Rene Cruz, Jr. Designer
Photos: Adrian Oradean
Client: Sol Glastein, Simple Simon, owner
Mark Zuckerman, Simple Simon, dir. of operations

Another visual solution to the problem of limited space was to maintain a 12' ceiling height. With loose fixtures and the "food court" kept at a low profile, sight lines were opened to view the perimeters where the merchandise lines the walls. Fluorescents and incandescent lights were mixed to create an overall warm environment. A suspended light rail mirrors the "food court" beneath and also adds to the decor of the store. At the perimeters the fascias were signed in neon to explain the different classifications of merchandise.

Simple Simon found its niche: "Between a convenience store and a gourmet food shop — with down-to-earth prices."

Frattelli Cangiano

MANHATTAN, NY

Design: Herb Ward Assoc., & F. Vando Design Group, NY

An existing building in Soho was completely redesigned into a small food shop that recalls "the old-world, open air markets of Europe." The entire store, — all 2500 sq. ft. of selling space is on view from the entrance. The aroma of freshly ground and brewed coffee is joined with the smell of the breads and cakes being baked in the bakery below and together they serve to entice the shopper and lead her/him through the U-shaped loop of the

**Francisco Vando: Desigrner & Job Captain
(formerly with Herb Ross Assoc., NY)
Client: Lou Cangiano, Sr., owner**

store's layout. The service areas are on the left, the produce, dry goods and beverages are on the right, and the small unassuming checkouts are at the end of the tour.

Above the center service area is a pair of ceiling vaults — reminiscent of the shopping arcades in old, European street markets, which tend to lower the ceiling in this area, and hopefully conjure up images of town square markets, — of individual booths or stands and the personal service one associates with these vendors.

Incandescent lights are used to highlight the produce, — to enhance and enrich their color while specialty lights are introduced for functional reasons and to extend the "European" imagery. A full time food stylist is responsible for the presentation of all the products in the store. The store's logo, colors, uniforms, and details down to the smallest bag were all part of the total design package.

Draegers Supermarket

LOS ALTOS, CA

Design: Boulton Design Group, Carmel Valley, CA

The Draeger family has been providing food and produce for over sixty years and this store, their second supermarket, of 17,000 sq. ft. is located near Stanford University. They had this store updated so that "the epicurean experience of grocery buying could be carried into a new realm of gourmet food shopping." The designers have provided an up-scaled setting for the fine food that is immediately apparent with the sleek black and white checkerboard floor, and the lustrous black checkout counters. Even the illuminated black cubes that identify the checkout stations are styled and stylish.

The ambient lighting is low-keyed and subdued so that the decorative and accent lighting readily stand out. Pictured left, in Produce, the viewer immediately sees the neon graphic on the black ceramic tile wall, — then the shopper's eye is led down to the bright exposure of the produce which is more than amply lit by the hidden fluorescents. The mirrored back wall of the case adds some reflected light which then pours out onto the aisle where it enhances the ambient light coming from the handsome pressed glass pendants with incandescent lamps.

The frozen food area is located in the middle of the store and is the last stop before going to the check-out counters. It makes a dramatic focal point for the store with the gleaming cases facing each other under the two glowing rows of fluorescents that light up the pinkish ceiling. The pink cast glows down past the assemblage of live plants on the cases down onto the diagonally laid black and white squares. To either side of this "grand allee" are gondolas of dry groceries. Along the perimeter walls are the dairy area, self-service meat and cheese, the meat and fish departments and the deli and prepared foods. All are displayed in an atmosphere that is both fun to be in and exciting to be a part of.

Neon Graphics: Designed by Michael Boulton, executed by Comet Neon and Signage
Lighting: MR16 tracks and fixtures: Halo incandescent pendant fixtures: D'lights
Tiled Walls and Soffits: Ceramic Tile by Villeroy & Boch
Photos: Jensen Photographics
Client: The Draeger Supermarket, Los Altos, CA

Breadstiks

LOS ANGELES, CA

Design: CDI Designs, Inc., Riverdale, NY

The designers were called in by R& S Oil — an oil company — to create a 4500 sq. ft. up-scaled food shop in an existing structure. The shop is located in the affluent Westwood Village section of West Los Angeles, only streets away from a convenience store also designed by CDI Designs, — for the same client. The client recognized a definite need for a food store in that location that would offer most of the basic convenience items as well as the new everyday items of the 1990s, — perishables and quality prepared foods. Though produce was not originally in the merchandise mix, it did become a featured department — up front at the entrance — in the final design. The layout overcomes the long, narrow configuration of the space and the gondolas are laid out under the overhead neon "wave" that draws the shoppers through the store.

The neon wave not only adds to the excitement of the space, it also becomes a distinctive "signature"

**Client: R&S Oil Company
Los Angeles, CA**

motif that also appears on the packing materials and shopping bags. In the middle of the store is a spectacular, custom designed salad bar that signals the store's commitment to fresh quality food, just as the whole store's look was designed to impart an impression of freshness, cleanliness and service.

Glass blocks, behind the fountain drink counter, suggest an up-scaled look for this area and avoids the stereotypical convenience store appearance. The low ceiling, at the front end of the store, is neutralized

by the use of polished aluminum which tends to affect the look of greater ceiling height. Throughout the store the square is used as a unifying motif. It not only appears in the previously noted glass blocks area, it is checker-boarded on the gray and white tile floors as well as on the white and red accented wall pictured on the lower left.

The designers not only developed the name Breadstiks, they also created the logo which is interpreted in neon over the deli counter.

Park 'n Shop

HONG KONG

Design: The Watt Group, Toronto, Ont., Canada

The Canadian-based architects were invited to reposition this chain of Park 'n Shop food stores in Hong Kong. Most of the stores range in size from 6000 to 10,000 sq. ft. and are located on heavily trafficked streets where space is more precious and more expensive than it is in New York City. The Watt Group studied the "traditional customer" and her shopping habits in the pre-design, strategic design process.

The layout, the lighting, the coloration and the design elements used

in this prototype store were all influenced by the cultural factors and the shopping habits and preferences of the customers. The store is overly bright in fluorescent light. Lowered luminaires make a bold pattern across the store and tend to "hide" the HVAC units that snake above the selling space. Dropped bands of red lacquered grills serve to delineate areas or shops and in addition to the color they carry the signage, — in three languages, over the specialized areas. Ceramic tiles cover the walls and floors for color and cleanliness.

D'Agostino

MANHATTAN, NY

Design: The Watt Group, Toronto, Ont., Canada

we sell kosher and
non-kosher food.
no carriages, no pets.
check all shopping bags
with manager.
shoplifters will be
prosecuted.

D'Agostino is a family owned chain and the Manhattan-based food shops are Yuppie Havens. The Watt Group was invited to develop a model for sites that would take up between 7000 and 10,000 sq. ft. of prime real estate in up-scaled, affluent areas where shoppers look for and expect quality and service. The designers evolved a strong graphic look for the stores and through the use of giant photo murals, the striking red, green and black bands and banners, and the neon signage they were able to create a distinct look for their client.

The floors are boxed off with white tiles outlined with black, and the pattern creates an easy-to-follow traffic pattern. Fluorescent luminaires are dropped over the perimeter specialty shops and they are masked by the striped fascia. Pendant incandescents, over the aisle, also help solve the problem of low ceiling heights. The neon signs and graphics solve the identification needs where space is severely limited and there is a heavy specialist penetration. The resulting effect is pleasing to the particular and very selective shopper identified with D'ags.

The Market Basket

FRANKLIN LAKES, NJ

Design: CDI Designs, Inc., Riverdale, NY

What started out as a successful catering business in an affluent area of northern New Jersey developed — due to customer demand — into a small retail store that eventually expanded into this 12,000 sq. ft. store. An existing market was completely renovated and half the space is still devoted to the catering business, and the other part is retail space. The store needed to project the "high quality and dedication to service that customers had come to associate with the Market Basket." The result is, as the designers state, "food retailing as theater" with stage-like settings for the butcher department and the dramatic use of lighting to accentuate special areas.

The store is concentrated almost entirely on high quality perishables with a limited selection of gourmet grocery items and candy. Fresh prepared foods, meat and bakery are the stars in the production. An order desk is conveniently located so that customers can arrange catering service.

The color scheme mixes strong primary colors with more muted,

post-modern tones, and the materials and textures are mixed with flair. Just as materials and textures are contrasted, so are traditional design elements played against more contemporary ones. The checkerboard wall tiles are reminiscent of by-gone, "good old" days, but the light is sharp and high-tech. Note the interesting lighting configuration on the produce, below, which combines fluorescent luminaires with tracks of spotlights.

Black is freely used as a contemporary, sophisticated accent and it is balanced with lots of crisp white. Natural woods are used as well as chrome, — again the mix and match of textures and periods to create an overall up-scaled setting for knowledgeable shoppers. The designers also created the store's logo and on the exterior facade it glows. The black letters contain neon which reflect onto the back wall and creates a halo around each letter.

Harbortown Market

DETROIT, MI

Design: Design Fabrications, Inc., Troy, MI

Located on the river, in downtown Detroit, is this 12,000 sq. ft. store. It is one of the many new projects started by the impetus of the Renaissance Center, and it is tuned in to the steadily growing population of in-towners who are settling in to the up-priced apartments and condominiums that are going up. The designers created the up-end logo and the look for the store which appears more spacious than it actually is. The black and white basic color scheme supports the sophisticated look.

The floors are covered with white vinyl tiles accented with squares of pale gray. The black and white cases are designed to go with the black and white signs that serve as product identification. A cool, pale teal color is added to the neutral palette as an accent, and the white walls over the perimeter shops are graphically enhanced with lettering that is both informative and decorative. Interspersed between the repetitive words are large appropriate murals of food being offered below.

The main source of lighting for the market are metal halide lamps in pressed glass pendants hung down from the corrugated metal ceiling way up above. Rows of fluorescent tubes are used to supplement the HID lamps, and they are located closer to the products.

All perimeter cases are self il-luminated with fluorescent tubes. Neon is used for special signage or product identification. The pale teal sound baffles that diagonally cross over the store also add a touch of color and tend to camouflage the HVAC units that fill the upper reaches of the structure.

Presidential Market
PRESIDENTIAL TOWERS, CHICAGO, IL
Design: Schafer Associates, Oakbrook Terrace, IL

"With increasing numbers of people moving back to the city, the Habitat Co. built a new apartment complex aimed at the young urban professional. The complex is called Presidential Towers and we were selected to design a supermarket within the retail mall. The objective was to design a supermarket for the up-scaled, time-pressed, urban dweller with emphasis on 'boutiques' of specialty foods; a one-stop food store in an apartment complex of 2400 units."

In planning the store it was important to move the shoppers through the 13,000 sq. ft. space in a controlled manner, — to expose "boutiques" like Floral, Produce, Ethnic

For Schafer Assoc.:
Ronald H. Lubber, V.P., partner in charge
Barry Vinyard, Planner & Designer
Consultants: Visual Communication Group,
Schafer Assoc.
Space frame: Robert Assoc., Inc., Chicago
ASI Sign Systems: Chicago, IL
Client/Owner: Habitat Co./Bockwinkel Enterprises Inc.
Photos: Jim Norris

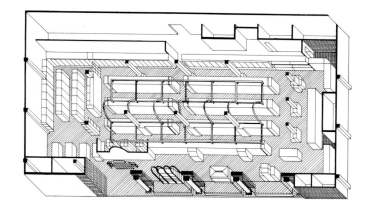

Foods, Bakery, Deli, Seafood and Liquor, while maintaining easy access to general grocery and non-perishable goods. Thus, the boutiques were arranged around the general grocery, — at the perimeters, and the glass front specialty shops spread out across the unusually wide mall frontage. The shoppers complete the circuit and check out at the single mall entrance.

The name Presidential Market suggests both formality and casualness. A logotype was developed with the formal emphasis in the type and arrangement of "Presidential," while a more relaxed, brush-stroke type was selected for "Market." For colors, the designers chose taupe ceramic floor tiles and the white wall tiles were accented with teal details.

The interior plan and design was orchestrated with a formal arrangement of alcoves for each boutique, with lowered ceilings, intimate lighting, individual fixture designs and graphic elements, — each shop was given a unique identity. The general grocery area is open with an exposed ceiling, vaulted space frames, and enhanced with festive banners. HID lighting helps express the desired open-air market quality. Moving signs, and the many scents and smells all contribute to making this an exciting food experience.

Zagara's

MARLTON, NJ

Design: Paul Purkalns, NY

Zagara's marketing and design strategy was to have a store that shoppers would classify as a "gourmet's delight." Thus, the designer was to create an interior that would stand apart from the traditional gourmet store, and the concept that evolved blended high-tech with the flair and freshness of the colors of Southern California. Space is limited in this 18,000 sq. ft. operation, and the building was constructed with clerestory windows twenty feet off the ground in the central space and with skylights over where the produce would be placed. A general lighting scheme that "created a secondary spatial plane" was devised and design accents were created by taking traditional fixtures and building materials and using them in innovative and unexpected ways. Since the building also had an exposed joist system, areas were accented with lighting and perforated steel. The entrance "chandelier" was made up of four intersecting I-beams with cord suspended pin spots set at varying heights, and it is a dramatic example of the designer's concept of making the usual—unique.

Pinks, peaches and aquas abound in a white environment that is

Architect: Kenelstein,
Timber, Danton & Jones
Contractor: Zagara Assoc.
Metal Work: Mike Dinardo
Space Cube: Integrated Ceilings
Client: The Zagara Family
John Zagara, co-owner

underscored with black. The unusual color feeling (for New Jersey) and the high-tech/California attitude — with Art Deco overtones — makes an impactful statement out front on the facade. The stepped motif of the windows is repeated inside the store (see opposite page) where pink and white ceramic tiles serve as dividers between specialty areas. The style and panache of the untraditional interior is most elegantly stated in the choice of type for the neon lettering used for the signage. Zagara's got what they wanted; a gourmet shop that has its own special look and attitude.

Ross Markets

MUNCIE, IN

Design: Design Fabricators Inc., Troy, MI

When Design Fabricators were asked to remodel this 20,000 sq. ft. store in Muncie, they conceived of the diamond-within-the-square as the motif, and the motif becomes evident in the new layout of the store. The grocery section became a diamond-within-the-square of the sales area, and the design motif reappears in the signage and decorative banners that are added.

The floor is patterned with big squares of gray tiles and the walls are finished to define the perimeter departments. Bands of neon and chrome are used not only to accentuate and delineate, — they also add sparkle and drama. The neon signage serves as well as for graphic enrichment over the merchandising areas as exemplified in the produce area (opposite page bottom) where the design takes on the look of a 50s diner. A variation of the chrome/neon fascia treatment is viewed below in the Deli section. Assorted colored diamonds-in-the-square banners add some extra color and sizzle in the freezer area.

The store is illuminated by a variety of light sources which include recessed metal halide lamps, fluorescent luminaires and strips behind the fascia, plus the dynamic glow of the neon in this carefully controlled lighting plan.

To Market, to Market, Designs for a Changing Consumer

The most memorable and successful food *retail designs* are the ones that *support* great *food retail ideas*. And the best ideas come from those retailers who acknowledge and understand the unprecedented change in today's consumer society. As designers, we must cater to our clients goals and needs by becoming aware of their customer's most current expectations and lifestyles.

Retailers and designers together must recognize that to serve a changing consumer society, you have to know a lot about the men and women who are changing it. A whole new set of values and priorities are redefining how today's consumers shop for food:

- The consumer market has become polarized into upscaled and downscaled segments. Retailers who have held the middle ground are either in trouble or changing rapidly. Consequently, food retail operations have been positioned into two dominant store types.

- The de-massification of the marketplace has produced niches and finite segments of consumer groups. Food operations are no exception to the fact that stores without clear focus or a specific target confuse their customers and consequently lose patronage.

- Luxuries are now affordable, yet this generation of consumers demands value and service to be included along with the luxury products they select. Food stores, likewise, must comply.

- Time has become the last luxury on earth and in a sense is the retailer's competition. Stores must make the shopping experience worth their customers' time. Food stores need to add efficiency, service and some creative marketing strategies to attract these time-pressed people.

In consideration of how consumer behavior has altered spending patterns, food operations have basically been positioned into two major types of stores.

The first type emphasizes *best-in-class of everything* . . . from gourmet specialty products to exotic perishables, organically-grown produce and specialty prepared foods. These stores highlight customer amenities, are exquisitely appointed and spacious.

Price and assortment are the main attributes of the second major food store type. These operations focus in on well stocked commodities and discount merchandise in an information-filled shopping environment.

The differences in both store types result from the polarization of the consumer market. It remains constant, however, that no matter what the format of the store, four common elements ultimately determine their success . . . *quality, convenience, value and service.*

It's time for food retailers to step back, examine, and determine that in order to prosper and grow their business, they must change along with the consumer. They must communicate a sensitivity to their customers' needs by providing nutritious, fresh, healthful, premium food products. To achieve differentiation, the business and the design of their environment should project the character, texture and "flavor" of the offerings.

Creative marketing strategies, in response to consumer lifestyles, will continue to initiate additional service and products such as menu and nutritional planning, selections of prepared foods, special dietary analyses, cooking demos and information, and home delivery services. The design of these stores must be as diversified as the marketing strategies.

Today's great food retail ideas and the great designs which support them take their signals from the changing consumer. The most successful stores are the ones that interpret constant change as endless opportunities.

Robert W. Schafer
Schafer Associates, Inc.

Chapter Two

20,000
To
40,000
Square Feet

Food Emporium

90th & BROADWAY, NYC

Design: A& P Store Design

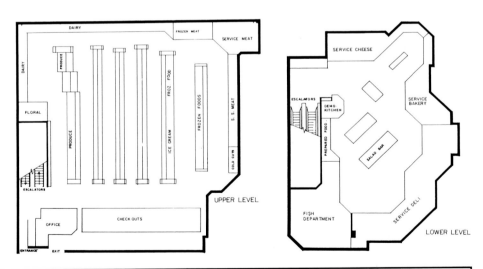

Client: The Greater Atlantic & Pacific Tea Company, NJ

"Some one made a store just for me, — someone has my kind of quality" — sings the jingle that is often heard sandwiched between Bach and Beethoven on the up-scaled radio stations in the New York City area. Food Emporium is that store and as the parent company, A& P, says, "—our Manhattan-based gourmet format has captured an upscale customer segment by offering exotic product mix and pleasant shopping atmosphere in tight urban environs." This, the second in the group is a two floor, "double-decker" store of 21,000 sq. ft., and an escalator moves the shoppers between the two levels.

On the store's street level is a complete grocery; an expanded produce market of exotic fruits and vegetables, — a butcher shop with both service and self-service section, — an expanded ice cream

department with more than one hundred twenty five varieties and flavors, and a floral shop. High speed scanning checkouts move the basket-loaded "yuppies" on their way efficiently and speedily. The lower level features a bakery with freshly baked products, — a NY style deli, — a seafood shop and a take-out bar. Also on this level is a large "World of Cheese" and a demonstration kitchen where gourmet classes are conducted. A very popular prepared foods area features a variety of exclusive hot and cold entrees.

The low ceilings are made to appear even lower with deep soffits, space frame canopies, and neon outlined arches spanning the aisles. The colors throughout are muted and subtle, — mostly gray and white and a checkerboard pattern of the two is a recurring theme. Fluorescents provide the general illumination while incandescents highlight the products on display.

Service is the name of this business which also provides telephone ordering and home delivery — which accepts major credit cards, and even makes postage stamps available at the checkout counter.

Mr. D's Food Market

INDIANAPOLIS, IN

Design: Commercial Interior Products, Inc., Fairfield, OH

Mr. D's operates five supermarkets in the Indianapolis area and with this, their Madison Ave. store, they wanted to give their customers and potential customers an up-to-date facility that is more reflective of the company's market niche and that will also keep that company in a growing and profitable position.

To reposition this 21,000 sq. ft. store and satisfy the client, the interior decor takes on a look of the past. The "old time feeling" of service and friendly help is recreated through the use of stained oak trim,

oak case fronts, floral print vinyl wallcoverings, traditional style awnings with hand painted graphics, brass lighting fixtures and screened banners. Even the service meat area has an oak finish which recalls the old ice houses that were found in meat markets before modern refrigeration. To accent the profusion of wood, burgundy and green are added for richness.

In contrast, the core of the store still conveys a simple, lower-price image which is what the client desired. The floor of this core area is covered with white vinyl tile while the perimeter shops are accented with color coordinated tiles. The main service area has custom designed ceramic patterns which border the cases. Energy saving metal halide fixtures are used in the open joist ceiling over the core area. The lower perimeter areas have recessed 2x4 fluorescent fixtures with para-cube lenses to provide subdued lighting levels. The walls are all lighted from recessed troughs which supply a bright image to the perimeter shops.

Miller's Supermarket

NORTHEDGE S/C, EATON, OH

Design: Commercial Interior Products, Fairfield, OH

The Miller's objective in their supermarket and shopping center expansion was to project an image of stability, integrity and show their continued involvement with Easton. For more than fifty years, the growth of the community has been essential to the Miller family and they asked the project team to plan for the 1990s but still keep a firm hold on the company's roots and heritage. During the expansion of the store to its present 21,400 sq. ft. size, the store remained open and customers were serviced.

The materials used emphasized a consistent warm combination of quarry tiles, natural oak trim, heavy duty vinyls and ceramic tiles on the back walls of the service shops. Natural oak was used to trim the ceramic tiled soffits and neon signage was placed over the tiled soffits to enhance the look of the area and be consistent with the

whole Miller's shopping experience. The patterned ceilings were treated with 2x4 troffer lights using paracube louvers to accentuate each areas product presentation.

The beverage and snack alcove was carpeted, and the darkened ceiling was fitted with track lighting to light up the product selection. This made a dramatic change from the general sales area just beyond where cost effectiveness required that the existing metal ceiling and strip fluorescents remain. The upper walls of the perimeter and the interior soffits were treated with a unique painted spectrum color pattern moving from light to dark at the ceiling. Eventually, the ceiling in the core area will be painted the dark color of the spectrum band and pendant metal halides will replace the fluorescent fixtures.

The traffic is directed towards the

service areas from the central core. Departmentalization is achieved through the use of custom colored wall vinyls framed with stained oak. Different treatments of machined oak trim and machined oak laps — with inlaid brass laminates — continue the special look of the service shops. The combination of lighting, wood treatments, and color invites the shopper to move from one product to the next.

The checkout sector, on the opposite page, welcomes the customer with a spectacular plenum of directed light through paracube louvers wrapped in the ten rows of natural machined oak with a bronze mirror reveal on the exterior and bottom surface. Miller's has brought a new excitement to this mostly rural farming community of which the family is so much a part.

Client: Miller's Supermarkets
C.E.O.: Robert Miller
Pres.: Timothy Miller

The Market Place at Foodtown

WARREN, NJ

Design: Arnold Ward Studios, NY

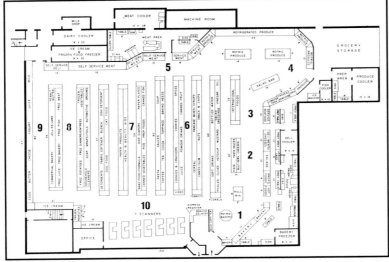

This 21,500 sq. ft. store is the first store for Bob Panzenhagen, and this is his dream come true. "I wanted to create a real specialty store in terms of prepared foods and gourmet items, but still provide all the basic groceries." Believing that today's consumers are looking for more than the conventional supermarket, he worked closely with the designers and with his wife, Nancy, in the design of the store's layout, and decorative concepts. Together they turned a former A& P store into this stylish operation.

The dominant look of this sophisticated shop is the dynamic black and white pattern that im-

Client: Bob & Nancy Panzenhagen
Quotes: Article appearing in
Progressive Grocer, Aug. '88

mediately suggests class, elegance and smart styling. The floor is covered in a bold checkerboard of large black and white boxes. The white tiled walls are banded with smaller black/white checkerboards of ceramic tiles. Overhead, the ceiling is patterned with glazed "skylights" that fill the spaces below with bright illumination, while some areas are "dropped," painted black and enlivened with an occasional square of fluorescent light. Ribbed, pressed glass downlights add a warm glow over the prepared foods and spotlights enhance the color. Natural oak and satin chrome are used to complement and accent the black and white surfaces.

To turn the clients merchandising and design concepts into a tangible reality required using state-of-the-art materials and creative solutions. Instead of actual marble, a faux marble made of a foam material combined with a formica laminate provides the desired richness in signage over the perishable cases, and where weekly price specials are a way of business,—a chalkboard is centered on the signs above the dairy and ice cream cases.

Alfalfa's Market

DENVER, CO

Design: Communication Arts Inc., Boulder, CO

Designed to showcase the cornucopia of natural foods it contains, the new Alfalfa's Market is a 22,000 sq. ft. flagship store which sets the standard for future locations planned by Natural Horizons, Inc.

The designers attempted to create a shopping environment that would be markedly different from those found in other food stores. Since the "natural foods" positioning is unique, the setting would have to

Client: Natural Horizons, Inc.
Photos: Greg Hursley

44

45

reinforce that specialness. To achieve their goals, the designers carefully planned product adjacencies, coordinated graphics, and they used the kiosks set up for food demonstrations and the display of specialty foods for the focal points in the design.

Using a palette of gentle southern California colors, the designers patterned the floor in a plaid of rose beige, salmon, aqua and pale blue. The same colors are used in the signage throughout the store. Typical of the kiosks created for the store is the one shown on the left. Under a spaceframe canopy is a light color laminated demonstration counter complete with cooking sur-

face and sink. The graphic signs above identify the demonstration area with "What's Cooking," and suspended from the canopy are white metal lamp shades with incandescent lamps that light up the counter tops.

The Herbs Boutique is set out under a skylight and sits on a rose beige floor. The woodworking and cabinetry are finished in off-white and accented with the rose tone. Each specialty area was specifically designed to accommodate its individual management, operation and display requirements. In Herbs, the classic-inspired woodworking has been divided into bins which accept the herb containers, and the free standing counter, up front, is used for the weighing and packaging. Spotlights in the ceiling provide the extra light that is needed here.

Throughout, lighting was carefully planned, area by area, to show off the products and also maintain the same pleasant warm, relaxed ambience.

47

Bristol Farms

SOUTH PASADENA, CA

Design: McClellan Cruz Gaylord and Assoc.

The owners of Bristol Farms selected this South Pasadena site in the Fair Oaks and Grevelia Center because of the area's affluence and the location's accessibility directly off the Pasadena Freeway. The exterior is high-tech and features concrete blocks, sandblasted concrete columns and beams, as well as curved, dark plexiglas canopies that are lit from within.

On the interior of the 22,000 sq. ft. store it is all quite different. Here it is "old fashioned" and charming and suggests a European marketplace filled with individual stands specializing in fine foods. Each department does operate as an individual store and provides customers with personalized selections and services.

Red brick floors are complemented by wood paneled ceilings in this courtyard setting. Spots are recessed into the ceiling and they illuminate the wide gracious aisles. Set out in the courtyard are oak

Clients: Irv Gronsky & Mike Burbank, Bristol Farms,
Palos Verdes, CA

tables and chairs, a sidewalk cafe and a coffee bar. The small shops that line the area are painted creamy beige and accented with teal and terra cotta.

The same intimate quality carries through into the grocery area. The gondolas are low in profile and small in scale and the profusion of red enameled metal pendant shades not only provide the ambient light, they add a decorative and festive feeling to the space.

In Produce, above, an 85 foot mural done in folk art style wraps around the area and it depicts scenes of South Pasadena and the San Gabriel Valley. The ceiling is beige with Douglas fir accents and the buff colored ceramic tiled walls are bordered with green.

The produce cases are red like the pendant shades and a high intensity, metal halide system was used to highlight the quality of the foods instead of the flourescents.

West Point Market

AKRON, OH

Design: F. Eugene Smith / Design Management, Akron, OH

Russ Vernon is the guiding light behind this successful, much talked and written about, and award-winning, 25,000 sq. ft. gourmet food store in Akron. "Our first and foremost function is to be of service to the customer. We want her to feel comfortable in the store." The store was designed for comfort — and convenience — and the lighting was acknowledged with a National lighting award for excellence.

Working closely with Russ Vernon, who knew what he wanted and what his customers wanted, and after studying the customers shopping habits, the designer came up with a new arrangement of aisles and departments which, in turn,

recommended a subtler use of color, form and more interesting types of lighting and light. Each food or floor display required its own unique lighting; crisp and fresh over the seafood to enhance the delicate color and the "just caught" mood, — and in the wine department an adaptable system of lighting depending upon the function that might be held in that space when it wasn't being used for sales. The ceilings were painted a dark color, and also lowered to seven different levels, — all to create a more human scale and break up the cavernous space. In some areas custom cedar grids were used and in others parabolic diffusers covered the fluorescent ceiling fixtures. Some incandescents

Minneola Tangelos 3 FOR $1⁰⁰
FLORIDA Grapefruit Pink or White 5 FOR $1⁰⁰

FLORIDA STAR RUBY GRAPEFRUIT 99¢

were recessed into the lowered ceiling while in other instances they were combined with pendant fixtures over the products in the cases and on the counters.

"We didn't want the West Point Market to look like any ordinary supermarket in any way and I think we were successful in achieving that. We looked for rational ideas to make the store work better, — not just for decoration but good ideas grounded in improved merchandising and improved function.

Thinking this way, we could adapt interior concepts not traditionally used in food markets." Probably because of his search for different approaches, F. Eugene Smith, the designer recently won an Edison in the lighting competition sponsored by General Electric and also a Halo award for the same, much-honored store.

Typical of the look and feel of West Point Market is this prepared food area. The almost white tiled floor picks up the light that is cast from the recessed incandescents in the dropped ceiling over the counter. More recessed lamps are added in the ceiling over the work space behind the counter. Spots, on

a track, light up the store logo and the wood framed chalk boards with the specials noted on them that are set against the rich, Pompeiian red back wall. The cases are low and lustrous — off white and polished chrome. The soffit is painted the same dark brown of the ceiling and both seem to disappear.

The gift items and baskets sit in a pool of dramatic, "specialty store" lighting. The baskets are meant to be filled with assorted products and

the excitement of watching fruits, nuts, candies and jams being layered into the unusual baskets is part of the store's living entertainment. Live plants and flowers — for sale or for show, are part of the store's decor — even to the flowers that are added daily to the customer restrooms.

The wine and liquor area suggests a fine wine celler with wall racks made of dark mahogany set against the deep red wall. An English tele-

phone booth, filled with flowers, adds an "old English touch" to the wine shop. Up front, under the rows of track lighting are wooden crates supporting a display of featured wines backed up with blooming plants and suggested filled gift baskets.

Posters and paintings were included in the design scheme along with one-of-a-kind, handcrafted fixtures and displayers. Russ Vernon really knows how to make his customers feel comfortable.

Shop'n'Bag

ATCO SHOPPING PLAZA, ATCO, NJ

Design: Off-The-Wall, Telford, PA

The upscale attitude of this new 25,000 sq. ft. store is apparent, up front, at the checkout area where the color scheme of mauve and white is first apparent. A dropped "skylight" over the counters fills the already well illuminated space with clear, bright light, and the horizontal signs add a rhythmic pattern that leads into the body of the store. The off-white tiled floor is patterned with geometric designs in different shades of mauve. The white counters are with the same color and the soffit is finished in a deeper shade of mauve that is pinstriped in white. Metal halide lamps are recessed into the acoustic tile ceiling to add to the clean, spacious feeling up front.

A diamond shaped motif is used as a recurring design element in the store. In the frozen food section, on the left, the diamond appears on the overhead banners that carry the signage. A series of half-diamonds or Vs, in mauve, become the decoration on the white soffit. Right, in the bakery area, the zigzag motif is repeated over the white tiled walls that are patterned with burgundy ceramic tiles. The signage and soffits that encircle the dropped "skylights" repeat the V design also. The burgundy color provides a subtle sparkle to the muted mauve that underscores all the white in the interior scheme.

On the opposite page, the produce cases that stand as islands in this area are set beneath inverted V skylights that flood the fruits and vegetables below with "daylight." Tracks of incandescent spots ring the skylights to add warm glowing light on to the display.

Bockwinkel's The Food Market

BURR RIDGE, IL

Design: Schafer Associates, Oakbrook Terrace, IL

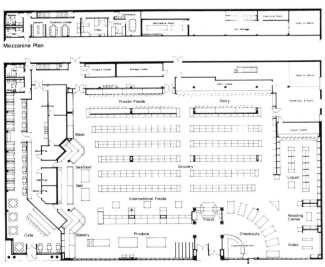

Mezzanine Plan

Client: Bockwinkel's, Inc.

"Bockwinkel's is a 25,000 sq. ft. market created to appeal to high income and 'established, affluent customers.' Our research (Schafer) indicated that the consumers in this locale are discriminating in their tastes and lifestyles, demanding in their desire for premium and quality products, and have a high regard for personal services and amenities."

To meet the requirements of such a customer, the designers developed a design strategy that matches the strength of the operator with the wants and needs of the shopper. A "Food as Fashion" attitude was created to enhance the presentation through the supermarket. A skylighted vestibule with an eight foot waterfall — at the entrance — sets the tone for the store. Mahogany and brass materials, as well as marble floor tiles, reinforce

the quality image of the premium products on display. End caps are crafted to appear as fine furniture and to create focal points for complete lines of gourmet products. An International Aisle, identified by large overhead banners, features special display tables and custom cabinets. Financial resources were used at the product display level where it can affect the shopper's buying decision. Cost savings were employed at the ceiling where the roof deck and structural joists were left exposed and suspended metal halide lighting became the major source of illumination.

The produce, bakery, floral and salad bar areas stretch across the

front of the store and are the first departments encountered by the shopper. Adjacent to the bakery is an expanded Deli which is accentuated by a lowered ceiling, pendant light fixtures, and marble wall and floor tiles. The checkouts are arranged in a semi-circle around customer service, and offers the luxury of space and customer comfort.

Acadia Market

MAUMELLE, AR

Design: Avery Graphic System, Merrillville, IN

Richard Robinson, store designer for Acadia Markets has a philosophy on store design for supermarkets. He believes that "when you enter a conventional supermarket it should be a destination within itself,—not just a place to purchase food or related items. The design should be open to the outside environment,—immediately establishing a sense of place."

The design for this 25,780 sq. ft. supermarket resembles a huge hacienda with its dominant interior skylight. "The intermingling of contemporary and southwestern architectural themes is as closely knit as the colors of Arkansas mountains and roaming hills" and the design did have to fit in with the design in-

Client: Acadia Markets, Richard Robinson, Store Engineer, Avery Graphic System Steven Chastaine, Director of Design

tent of the community, — and still be adaptable to other Acadia Markets across the state of Arkansas. "I wanted the decor and specialty departments to dominate the customer's view as they entered the store so that the customer could visually capture the depth of products and services offered in one sweeping glance," says Steve Chastain, director of Design for the Avery Graphic System group who was called in to decorate and sign the space. He believes that it is this design element that also promotes the traffic flow in and out of the sales area.

Changing lighting techniques, colorization taken from a carefully planned Art program, along with the use of neon and awnings were the key decorative design elements used to complement the products and the architecture.

Appletree Market

AUSTIN, TX

Design: Avery Graphic System, Merrillville, IN

"Catering to an upscale market of young professionals in the affluent Westlake Hills area of Austin, the emphasis was placed on a store design that would provide for a well lit, easily identified environment that would also enhance the whole fresh image of Appletree Markets."

To get that wholesome, up-scaled look, the designers resorted to a color scheme of contrasting black and white plus rose beige and turquoise. In the photo above, The Frozen Foods area is placed in front of the Seafood Shop which is one of the specialty shops to be found in Appletrees. The floor is boxed off in a bold, black and white checkerboard

of vinyl tiles, and the white enameled freezer cases are banded in
black. For the Seafood Shop, the
awning sets the color palette; aqua
tiles are set into the rose beige tiled
wall in back and a coral stripe accents the awning.

There is a minimal use of graphics
and signage but where and when
they are used they do make a strong
decorative statement. The various
areas of the store are color keyed
and the strong red panel behind the
Deli sign designates this shop as
part of the meat area. The marigold
yellow serves to distinguish the
cheese and dairy section.

The main aisle is white tile and the
black/white checkered pattern is used to highlight the specialty shops
off the main track. A small sit down
cafe, on the far right sits on the
checkered floor. In the Deli area the
black and white motif is also used
for the fixtures and the tile on the
rear wall.

The step down areas — the soffit
space between the ceiling and the
lowered specialty shops—were
given an architectural quality that
at the same time opened up areas
for the bold departmental signs.
This 27,760 sq. ft. store also has a
pharmacy, a florist, a complete
bakery and a salad and juice bar.

Funari's Thriftway

GIBBSTOWN, NJ

Design: Commercial Interior Products, Fairfield, OH

The Funari's have been in business and have been catering for over 60 years to a small, NJ community that has a high concentration of Italian descendants. They have gone from the traditional, small mom-and-pop corner grocery store to this full-fledged 30,000 sq. ft. supermarket. Always, in working with the store designers, the clients stress the importance of creating an atmosphere that shows the customer an up-to-date store, and still provides reminders of the past services that Funari customers have come to expect.

In working with the Funaris, the designer came up with certain overall concepts that would affect the general color and feeling in the store. All cases and the floor tiles were to be white, and an extensive use of oak was made. Personalized department signs were created like "Frank's Produce" and "Mom Funari's Deli-Bakery." There was to be an emphasis on the personal touch — on the friendly, neighborly feeling that the clients wished to promote.

Mom Funari's Deli-Bakery was to get special emphasis. To achieve a different look, the oak was eliminated and decorative lighting was combined with the elliptical signs used in this area (see below). The rich Pompeiian red soffit carries the oval signs and extending off the soffit, between the signs, are red metal shades with incandescent lamps. Troffer fluorescents are patterned into the dropped 10' ceiling. The general ceiling height over the grocery gondolas is 12'. The ceiling over the perimeter shops were lowered for emphasis and to achieve a friendlier feeling. Metal Halides were also included in the overall lighting plan.

The result: a modern supermarket personalized with a home-town feeling.

F.J.'s Blackhawk Market

DANVILLE, CA

Design: Bolton Design Group, Carmel Valley, CA

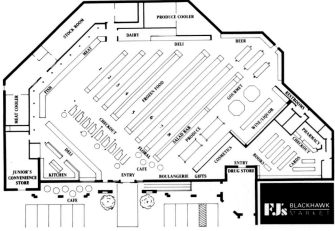

**Client: Frank J. Straface,
owner of F.J.'s Blackhawk Market**

Located in Danville, 30 miles east of San Francisco is this unique store that attracts its customers with live piano music and then relaxes them with a leisurely, complimentary cup of coffee. The coffee is the house blend and subtley serves to let the shopper know that there is a coffee area in this lively, pulsating store. The market is part of the Blackhawk Plaza which is a complex of stuccoed structures enriched with arches, rounded columns and washed over with soft, southwestern colors. Frank Straface, the market's president, says, ''We want to be known for customer service and one stop shopping. We tried to create an en-

vironment based on respect for our customers." In addition to atmosphere, the customer is offered the best available product at competitive prices.

A pianist, dressed in a tuxedo, is located in the store's cafe and plays a grand piano—shades of Nordstrom's. The music blends in with the up-scaled design motifs introduced by the Bolton Group. The floor is black and white tiles laid out in a giant checkerboard streteched across the aisles to make them look even wider. Everywhere there is the glint and sparkle of polished brass set off against the gleaming black tiles and mirror-like surfaces. Even the shopping carts

are elegant and are designed with panache; black and brass to harmonize with the store interior. Simple, Doric-like columns of natural poplar are used as a repetitive, unifying design element. Left, in Seafood and Meats, the columns create a colonnade behind the lustrous black cases up front, and the stepped up black design on the rear wall is framed by the columns.

A trellis arcade of the poplar wood serves to set off the produce area as a specialty shop. The cases are black banded in brass for an extra touch of refinement, and even the lazy circling fans combine the black and brass in keeping with the nostalgic trip to by-gone elegance.

Further back in this area one can see the white square umbrellas that serve as canopies over feature tables.

Throughout this 30,000 sq. ft. store the shopper is comforted and lulled by the live plants often in terra cotta planters and the black lattice framework that unifies parts of the store. The store is subtley lit. In addition to hidden fluorescents that wash the walls and ceilings, there are recessed incandescents and the antique-looking, brass and ribbed crystal pendant lamps. An occasional band of neon is used for emphasis and the MR16s are added for the sparkle and life they impart.

Ito-Yokado Co. Ltd.

NARASHINO-SHI, CHIBA, JAPAN

Design: N/A

This, the largest supermarket in Japan is located in a suburb of Tokyo. The food department covers almost 31,000 sq. ft. and it is part of a hypermarket that also carries apparel and household supplies. The store is an interesting blend of contemporary, ultra-today methods and materials combined with traditional Japanese customs and selling practices. The lighting, throughout, in true Japanese shopping style, is light and bright with fluorescents with incandescent spots supplementing where the product or produce needs an extra lift or sparkle. In addition to the meat, dairy and packaged products, there is an

abundance of pre-packaged, ready-to-go meals, and spices and seasonings are available in bulk.

Traditionally dressed employees stand behind some of the counters to prepare and/or serve the food, — customized to the shopper's request. In the freshly baked foods area, the saleswomen wear simple white smocks with matching head-coverings. The Bakery is a contemporary, glass enclosed shop and in the fruit and vegetable section, the shopper can have her selected produce blended into a refreshing drink to enjoy there — or to take home.

Centre Supermarket

TOLEDO, OH

Design: CDI Design Inc., Riverdale, NY

The project involved expanding and renovating an existing store for an independent supermarket operation in Toledo. The design process had to take into account the timing and phasing of the construction so that new departments could be operational while the existing store space was remodeled. The square footage was being increased from 23,000 to 32,360. The expansion involved the addition of a number of service departments including seafood, bakery, deli, and cheese and also a small snack bar and a florist. Customers enter the store near the bakery where they are greeted with the appealing smell of freshly baked

goods. From there they are directed to the deli and produce department (above) along the right hand perimeter.

To define and dramatize the produce department, a skylight was simulated with fluorescent tubes set in the plenum above the frosted glass framework. The rest of the area is lit by fluorescent luminaires spaced in the dropped ceiling. A rich brown color cuffs the soffit.

The deli area is distinguished by the bright red ceramic tile on the back wall and the wedgwood blue band

that outlines the lower part of the soffit. The pendant milk glass shades direct the incandescent light down onto the meats displayed in the white enameled cases which are also accented with the blue color.

The self-service meat area is white with a band of blue on the floor. Behind the low self-service cases is a long, exciting photo mural of the product set against a black background. As in the other perimeter areas, the signing is understated and placed way up on the soffit, just under the ceiling.

Natural wood walls and white are combined in the liquor shop and the flower shop next to it. A dropped ceiling brings the light closer to the products on the low gondolas and recessed high hats provide the ambient light for the area.

The overall white environment is pleasant and seems to expand the newly expanded store even more.

Martin's Supermarket

ERSKINE PLAZA, SOUTH BEND, IN

Design: Commercial Interior Products, Fairfield, OH

"Big—Bold—Dramatic—and RED! These were the words given to us in the preliminary design concept meetings with the owners. This store (34,500 sq. ft.) replaced an old and aging store located just across the street from the new store. The owners wanted to maintain their old customer base yet draw from those around the store who were not shopping there. Thus, we had to change the image but not to the point that the store lost its identity to long time customers."

The general food market is located in the center of the store under a 15 foot ceiling. Recessed fluorescent

**Client: Martin's Supermarket, South Bend, IN
Robert E. Bartels, president
Dan Baily, V.P., operations**

strip lighting provides a bright, cheerful atmosphere. This central area is ringed by a 5 foot soffit which becomes the background for the bold red and white checkered pattern wall vinyl. This strong pattern can be seen from anyplace in the store. The ceiling was lowered to 10 foot around the perimeter to create a more intimate and personal feeling for the service shops located here.

The owners agreed to the design concept of "individual shops" around the general food core. In addition to the lowered ceiling height, the lighting is subdued by the use of

2x4 trouffer light fixtures with para-cube lens. Thus, the products displayed here pop out in a halo of light. Each merchandise area makes use of slatwall, wall vinyl and brushed aluminum trim. Specialty shops such as the bakery, fish and deli have neon signage and art graphic neons for identification. The neon areas are bordered with a custom tubular trim with "wet look" vinyl overlays. The cheese shop gets special attention by the tubular light system which makes it stand out from the surrounding subdued lighting. The same tubular light system is used in the frozen foods area, and since the lights are suspended from a higher ceiling, it provides a decorative accent to the department. The red glow from the backlit awning with the dynamic lettering gives the meat area its own unique stamp. Hanging from the 17 foot high, red tiled ceiling, are large red and white checkered banners which locate the thirteen checkout registers, and the high ceiling adds to the feeling of spaciousness, — where it counts.

Gerrard's Food City

TORONTO, ONT., CANADA
Design: Omniplan/Miller Zell, Toronto

"We took the notion of 'street mer-
chants' — entrepreneurial shopkeepers — into the supermarkets
because the street-scape concept is
generic to the way people like to
shop," says Chester Niziol, president
of Omniplan/Miller Zell. And, with
the individual shopkeeper in mind,
and with the design concept of old
fashioned, small specialty stores as
the device, — the old becomes new
again in this refurbished 35,400 sq.
ft. store. The result has been most
satisfying. Shoppers seem to delight
in this street-scape approach over

the more traditional supermarket look.

Here the shopper finds that the "shopkeepers" wear different "uniforms" and they like the occasional park bench for just sitting down or the phone booth that reminds them of the calls they meant to make. The out-of-door city street feeling is reinforced by the different and individualistic signs over the "shops," the displays painted on the walls and the facades. There are even billboards over the shops, on the perimeter walls, that are rented out to product suppliers. For fun, the grocery aisles are given actual street names. To complete the city street concept there is a real hot

dog stand under a striped umbrella and also a popcorn stand.

The deli area is just down the "street" from the Market Garden (see previous page) which is centered under an elaborate two tiered white metal tube trellis that suggests an old European market with the glass panes removed.

The store front concept (next page) is promoted by the big graphic sign over the pitched roof line and the "windows." The striped awnings are a recurring theme on the "street" and they are also reminiscent of the striped pattern of neon tubes on the store's exterior facade. The basically white space is enriched with brick

red and yellow-gold. Just beyond, in the self-service packaged meat area, the wall units are the same bright red. The floor is off white vinyl tiles accented with squares of red.

What city street would be complete without a Pizza stand and here the stand is capped with a canopy of turquoise that matches the base of the stand. Paler aqua tiles are laid in the off white floor. The signs siz-

zle with neon and are set at several angles so they can be seen from different parts of the store. To the right of the Pizza stand, in the grocery area on Linton Ave. is a wide selection of pastas, tomatos, pastes and sauces, and cooking oils.

In addition to the large white globe lights that are used to suggest old street lamps, there are rows of spots strategically lined up on the ceiling, and emphasis lighting in or on each stand, shop or booth. The old time street lamps help attract the shoppers to the Boulevard, which is the checkout area, finished in gray.

The traffic pattern starts at the fifty foot tubular structure over the produce tables and moves clockwise. The pattern seems to end at the City Snack Bar which, like Deli City, is embellished with a red and white striped awning. Amy Lipton, writing about this store in Supermarket Business (April '89) calls this Gerrard design "Back to the Future" — and it's working.

Marui Imai Co. Ltd.

SAPPORO, JAPAN

Design: Chaix & Johnson, Los Angeles, CA

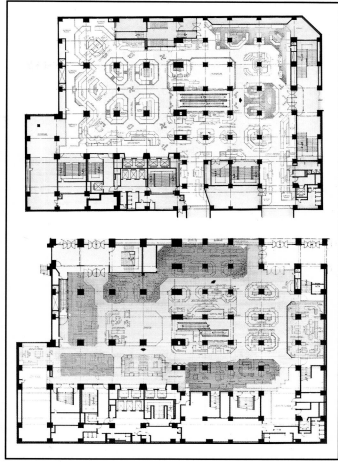

"Our design objective for this renovation was to create a very 'fashionable' urban department store, — a trendsetter, yet very refined. An important aspect in our planning solution was to develop easy customer circulation and to create a strong 'first impression' in each department." The last phase of the very extensive renovation of the flagship store of the Marui Imai Co. Ltd. were the two basement floors. The Japanese department stores are noted for their Food Halls which are usually located below the main floor entrance but on the level with the subway and people rushing to or from work. In addition to the standard and anticipated provisions, the halls are filled with the marvelous aromas of foods being freshly

prepared. All is neat, crisp and clean; the salespersons in white smocks with covered heads, — kneading, cutting, chopping, cooking and baking in full view of the shoppers. Throughout, small cafes and bars are set up for sampling and snacking.

The store planners design and style approach was to emphasize simplicity in a modern environment. Soft, as well as strong pastel colors were combined with textured and crazed tiles, and innovative architectural elements were created. The two floors shown here include Fresh Foods and Gourmet areas on Basement Level 1 (18,900 sq. ft.) and

Basement 2 (17,720 sq. ft.) is shared by grocery and confectionary. Together the area is 36,620 sq. ft.

To achieve their desired results and satisfy the clients needs, the designers focused in on two major elements. Of great importance is the easy identification of merchandise, and that had to be paired with easy customer circulation. To achieve either requires simplicity of design. The design should allow "the customer to focus in on the merchandise rather than have to sort through the design elements." Good lighting, of course, is vital to the success of the design. In this store, there is suspended fluorescent

lighting from the ceiling directly over the vendor areas which readily points out each individual vendor island. Spotlights are used not only to accent the merchandise but also add freshness and sparkle to the surrounding areas. To set up "easy customer circulation," the designers used color and light. The floor coverings define the aisles and traf-

fic areas. The lighting reinforces these patterns and has "the ability to draw attention and lead the customer through the vendor areas."

The Marui Imai food floors maintain the overall image created for the department store, and this is important to the client.

Clyde Evans Market

LIMA, OH

Design: Commercial Interior Products, Fairfield, OH

"Our philosophy of business is very simply to take care of all customers by offering them the best possible service. Most of all, Evans treats the customers like family so they will want to keep coming back. Evans endeavors to fill all our customers needs. We are a 'one-stop-shopping store'." With this credo foremost, the designers approached the layout for this new 39,200 sq. ft. store.

Looking to create a smart, stylish and up-scale image, the designers felt that the 18' ceiling would give the whole store a lofty, open feeling but not be so imposing as to frighten off the older shoppers who remembered the old store just

across the street. The central core of the store which contains the general food merchandise is under that high ceiling and it seems to suggest the image of "one-stop" shopping convenience. The area is lit with recessed fluorescent strip lighting to give a brighter look to the merchandise racks beneath the lamps. The entire perimeter of the general merchandise area is enclosed by a soffit design which provides an effective backdrop for the large scaled decor. There are oversized peaks and arches created with brushed aluminum trim and accented with graphic paint and wall vinyls. Within these peaks and arches that are spaced around the

**Commercial Interior Products: Thomas Huff, C.E.O.
Client: Clyde Evans Markets, Lima, OH**

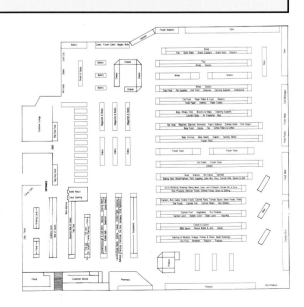

perimeter wall are neon graphics and/or signage that identifies the shops below as Meat, Deli, Bakery, Dairy, Pharmacy or Video. In the two specialty areas, illustrated above, the white tiled floor is gridded with an insert of red vinyl strips, and a similar red grid pattern on white backs up the neon signs in the architectural frames in the soffits overhead. In the Deli-Bakery areas, transluscent, back-lit, red awnings are lettered on in white and the floor fixtures and cases are finished in red enamel. In Meats, the counters are arranged into a saw-tooth design to invite the shoppers to come closer. These cases are white enamel accented in red.

A variety of ceiling patterns is evident in Clyde Evans. Above, the Produce department becomes a dramatic next-step-through the store. The graceful, fifty foot long arched skylight embraces the entire overhead view of this space and affects an atrium-like setting for the department. The simulated skylight also provides the fluorescent lighting that is necessary to sparkle the island displays of produce.

Over the frozen foods area, left, the long run of low, self-service cases is complemented by the cut-out cornered rectangle of red set in a white ceiling. Some 2x4 trouffer fixtures are highlighted in this area while long stretches of exposed fluorescent strip lighting are lined up on either side.

Lower left: in the foreground is the Pharmacy and beyond is the very important group of specialty shops. Note the recessed wall washer system that makes a halo around the upper part of the soffit.

This large supermarket still manages to be intimate, and combines big conventional supermarket convenience with small market comfort. Each of the individual specialty shops, under the perimeter soffit, has its own unique identity yet they blend with the others for a total design harmony.

Sav-A-Center

PHILADELPHIA, PA

Design: A& P Store Design Group

"Our Sav-A-Center concept represents a dramatically different supermarket alternative for our Philadelphia shoppers. Besides offering shoppers a unique shopping atmosphere, our new super stores also feature exceptional value, selection, quality and service. In addition to satisfying basic shopping needs, we have introduced many new service departments and an expanded variety of prepared and specialty foods — to make shopping even more enjoyable." Michael Bozza, V.P. of the Super Fresh of Philadelphia group said the above about the newly opened 39,800 sq. ft. store that is part of the ever growing Great Atlantic & Pacific Tea Company (A& P).

The store features a distinctive decor treatment that includes a vibrant green and white color scheme highlighted by large, full color murals illustrating the food products. The green border, over the products displayed on the perimeter wall cases, is designed to facilitate the ever-changing prices and noting of feature items. A light canopy, directly over it, serves to light up the price information on the products below. Green is also used to trim the wood covered wall cases.

In produce, below, the center island tables and the wall units are covered with country-style planks of knotty pine that not only suggest "country-freshness" and "down home goodness," but they also imply that the prices are realistic and competitive. To upscale that image — and also complement it, the green light canopies that circle the wall units, — the sign band below them and the large feature signs hanging over the island squares are all in the bold, easily recognized green that is a signature note in the

When
the Prices come down

overall design scheme. The overhead lighting illuminates the giant graphics that wrap around the wall.

To continue the country look and the homey comfort of the warmly lit store, the bakery floor is laid with brick and the perimeter shop, set underneath the overhanging graphics (right) is decorated with the green color. The on-the-floor feature tables of pine are located under wooden canopies that resemble garden trellises. They not only carry the fluorescent strip fixtures but also support the attached spots that warm up the products below.

In the grocery core of the store, long runs of fluorescent strips light up the aisles between the gondolas.

Store Designer's Challenge: A Supermarket for the 90's

"Designing a store" is a rather general statement. To be a complete designer in the food marketing industry is a more specific task. First, you must understand food merchandising and departmental distribution. The product, food, is the epitomy of the phrase "impulse buying." The designer must understand what motivates people to purchase this product.

If you think about it, food is one of the few products that is sold on a point-of-purchase display in its natural state, i.e., fish, produce, meats and dairy. This is why today's store designer's biggest challenge is to be a total environmental designer.

Let's start with lighting. A quality food market is the most difficult retail environment to light. Today it's not your typical 100 foot candle light box of the 60's and 70's, but multi-source lighting designed specifically for each department. The philosophy of the 90's and beyond is to light the product, not the ceilings or floors, with ambiant lighting for the walls. Just like a camera lens, your eye is drawn to the brightest light source. That source should be product, not a fluorescent light bulb. With today's technology, a retailer cannot use the old argument, "I must give up environment for energy efficiency."

Materials and colors are also important design factors. Color studies have shown that cool colors or neutrals are most desirable for the food market interior. Oranges, yellows, and reds are great for fast food restaurants, but they increase blood pressure and psychologically move people too fast through an environment. When the success of the store is based on the "impulse buy" in a profitable perimeter department, then color becomes a very important factor. If we had our choice on a color concept for a store, it would be grays, whites, and blacks. These tones allow natural products to be the color in the store and enhance merchandising creativity.

Because of the philosophy mentioned above, we feel that designs will become simpler, sleeker, and more sophisticated, allowing the store's merchandising to be the focal point.

If there is such a thing as absolute fact, this is it: "If the food store designer is not first and foremost a lighting expert, then he may as well sell shoes."

Thomas Huff, President
Commercial Interior Products, Inc.

Chapter Three

40,000
To
50,000
Square Feet

Abco Market

PHOENIX, AZ

Design: King Design, Inc., Eugene, OR

King Design, Eugene OR
Nancy Wade, Director of Design
Client: Abco, Ed Hill, C.E.O.

Abco was in need of an identity. They had an established clientele, — upper middle class to upper class, — and they required a visual image that would coincide with their niche in the market place. The stores were plain, — they lacked color and excitement, — they did not truly represent the Abco image or reflect their customers' taste level. The designers were brought in to create a more up-scale feeling, but not to the exclusion of the important middle-class shopper. In addition to a fresh, colorful and stimulating environment, the customer had to be reassured that she was getting the best quality for a good price. As a solution, a uniform contemporary graphic ap-

proach was taken for the basic wall decor. Within this approach, color arches served to divide the store into various departments. A warm, almost regal, color scheme of deep burgundy and light sand was adopted and presented against a crisp, white background. To unify the store, an accent band of black and white grid was added as a contemporary note.

The same black grid was repeated on the perimeter floor tiles. Almost all the cases were finished in almond to further unify the floor and also keep the sand/burgundy color scheme. However, in the deli and bakery shops, the European styled cases were custom matched to the burgundy of the walls. Awnings were used as a decorative note, — and a relief from the flat fascia.

Energy efficiency and long term, easy maintenance had top priorities in the development of the lighting plan. The client desired a light, bright and airy look and preferred

using standard fixtures to do the job. Thus, over the main grocery section strip fluorescents work efficiently, and the designers recommended painting the aluminum hoods that shield the tubes used over the checkout counters. Accent lights were used in some specialty shops and incandescent pendant lights also served as a visual divider,

and brass was added as a decorative note.

Neon was employed to serve as a sharp, stinging accent in the arched elements and also with the awnings. The overall effect is bright, light and airy, and the light level of 110 F.C. is maintained mainly with color-corrected fluorescents.

Gelson's Market

MARINA MARKETPLACE, MARINA DEL REY, CA

Design: Brown, Bunyan, Moon and More

The Gelson operation has come a long way since Bernard and Eugene Gelson opened their first supermarket in Burbank in 1951. Since then they have gone on to become a premier chain in the Los Angeles area with eight full-service, one-stop, shopping markets.

The new 40,000 sq. ft. Gelson's Market includes a gourmet coffee bar with a seating area where customers can enjoy the baked delicacies and prepared foods which are freshly made on the premises. A service deli features a 36 inch wok to prepare Oriental specialties, and the meat department has a full time butcher ready to specially cut meats as well as a self-service area. In addition, there is a salad bar with over 40 items, and a soup bar with several different selections daily.

Architect: Altoon & Porter
Client: The Gelson Company

The market is located on the lower level of the mall. Customers pass by a lovely fountain and enter into a spacious area with neon outlined vaulted ceilings that enhance the open, airy feeling. The store has a very contemporary look and there is a strong emphasis on pastel colors accentuated with bright complements. Ceramic tiles and natural oak are added for a quality touch.

Live plants grow beneath the triangular skylights that are located over some areas, and the same triangular motif is evident in the vaulted ceiling — outlined with red neon, shown on the opposite page. Smaller, red-outlined, inverted Vs carry the triangular shaped department signs.

The coffee bar is set beneath a dropped ceiling, and the counter and soffit are both finished with natural oak and white. Incandescent lamps light up the food in the cases and on the counter. Beyond is the sitting area.

With service as their main object, the Gelson Company is proud that their markets are laid out simply to shorten the time of the shopping trip and to speed their satisfied, upscaled customers through the checkouts.

A. &P.

The venerable old supermarket chain has become the New supermarket as it presents its new graphic-bright face to the public. Drawing on experiences learned in other 40,000 sq. ft. stores, the company and the designers have been able to create this striking new look with an improved layout, store design and lighting techniques, — and greater customer comfort and appeal.

The interior is sparkling light and bright — all black and white with handsome contrasting graphics calling out across long aisles to announce what is to be found along the perimeter walls. The lighting combines HID with incandescents for a pleasant overall effect that also enhances the color of the produce. The gondola lighting was "computerized" by the designers to provide even light levels to all shelves — top and bottom. At the checkout area a lowered ceiling and softer lighting creates a sense of intimacy to customer and employee.

Traditional signage is almost non-existant in this very graphic environment. Except for special event signs,

sale signs, and price identification, everything is said with pictures. In the Frozen Food area, shown on the left, the bold, black, cube-like soffits loom large and are readily seen from anywhere in the store. On each face is a simple drawing that indicates what type of frozen foods are stacked below, whether they be fish fillets or frozen dinners . . . According to the designer, Robert Gersin, "The environmental graphics should identify product and service classifications, provide decorative focal points consistent with the image and visually unify the store. In a supermarket there are often two kinds of communication needs; one for those who come to pick up a few items and for those doing their weekly shopping. The communications system must answer both needs, making the shopping trip as efficient and as pleasant as possible."

In the deli area, above, the striped belly in the ceiling seems to lower the ceiling over this counter and creates a more intimate feeling. The dramatic sweep also brings the recessed incandescent lamps closer to the prepared foods on display.

A& P is not only upgrading its image on the selling floor, — the company is also endeavoring to "elevate the quality standards and customer perception." Indeed it is a "Proud New Feeling" as the jingle goes.

Clemens Market

LIONVILLE CENTER, LIONVILLE, PA

Design: Off-The-Wall, Telford, PA

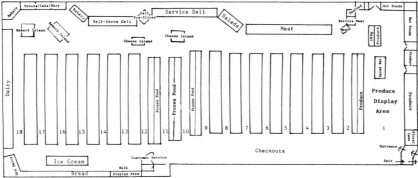

Client: Clemens Markets, Inc., Lansdale, PA

"The ceiling line of this 40,000 sq. ft. store was of particular importance to our client. Clemens wanted luminous ceiling panels, but they wanted them used in other than the traditional skylight approach." The design solution was to fabricate drop valances entirely of white, back-lighted, panels.

These drop valances follow the department perimeters of produce, bakery, deli, meat and seafood with a large area jutting out towards the front of the store to delineate frozen foods. Since the entire sales

area is laid out on an angle, this lighted irregular valance creates a dynamic focal point that is clearly visible from anywhere in the store. In The Butcher's Block (meat) area, the on-the-floor refrigerated cases are finished in bright blue and capped with matching illuminated canopies that feature fluorescent strip fixtures. The same blue appears on the perimeter cases and also serves as an accent band of the fascia above them.

The color scheme is basically "cool" — yet warm. The mauve to

aubergine color is the major strong color with blue assisting, and beiges and off-whites filling in the large neutral areas. The effectiveness of the illuminated valance is dramatically shown here, and the intricate "skylight" over the freezer cases makes a high point from which the trusses descend to carry the graphic signage. Metal halides serve the general sales area, and fluorescents, specified in the 3500 degree Kelvin range, were selected for color rendition in the service and perishable departments.

Bill's Supermarket

DALEVILLE, PA

Design: Off-The-Wall, Telford, PA

Client: Bracey's Supermarkets, Inc., Moscow, PA

The recent General Electric "Edison" award for outstanding lighting design, went to the designers of Bill's Supermarket, a 41,000 sq. ft. store located near Scranton, PA. It was a well-deserved honor for the Off-The-Wall design staff since almost all are I.E.S. certified in lighting design. In the sales area, HID lamps are used to provide the overall pleasant light, while in other areas fluorescents and incandescents are mixed to achieve the specially desired effects. At the checkout registers, above, eight foot box lights are suspended from the pale turquoise ceiling over the individual counters and the distinctive logo/graphic banners are done in shades of coral. The fascia behind is painted in beige and peach. The subtle, multicolored floor tiles complete the light open feeling for the store.

The lighting in the produce area, is provided by six foot box lights, accented with red stripes and capped with red triangular shapes with black mesh inserts. The red stripe and the black grid is repeated on the peach colored wall, — over the stacked produce, and black accents gleam on the pale peachy-beige cases. The same light neutral color is used on the feature squares on the floor which are outlined with natural wood. Suspended down from the ceiling is a white track with white housings for the spots that are used to highlight the merchandise on display. In the dropped ceilings, over the perimeter walls, one can see a row of recessed incandescents set into the gridded ceiling. The light colored floor is patterned with aqua and deep gray tiles.

The decor elements used in the frozen foods area over the aisles, and those in the checkout area are fabricated in circular and triangular designs. They also serve by carrying the signage.

Above, in the seafood area, white faced fabric awnings, trimmed with red sides, are set off from the red soffit. The Bill's logo is screened on the face of the awning. The back wall of the service shop is tiled in an eye-arresting yellow/green/black design on white tile. Floating over the free-standing island cases and feature areas are graceful white pendant shades with globe incandescent lamps. Note the recessed spots and fluorescent luminaires in the ceiling.

Pick 'N' Save

APPLETON, WI

Design: Commercial Interior Products, Fairfield, OH

"The owners expected it to be the biggest and best in town. They liked various ceiling heights, soffits, upscale treatments, neon and specially treated departments to accentuate the service orientation of the store." With a long list of "to-dos," the designers set about to turn this upscale, super warehouse store of 41,231 sq. ft. into an attractive food market styled in "low tech contemporary with some touches of conservatism." Roundy's store layout and engineering department planned the superwarehouse perimeter departments and equipment, but it was Tom Huff's task as C.E.O. and designer of Commercial Interior Products to create the selling ambience.

The designer's assignment was to create the decor/designs and plans

for the following: Lighting for the sales area, soffit location with construction details, flooring requirements for the sales area, wall and ceiling decor plans, as well as specifications for case colors, ceramic tiles in service areas and on walls, neon details plus all other decorative components.

For the flooring plan, four colors of 1/8th inch vinyl tile was specified with both 1″ and 2″ accent strips to be used throughout the store. American Olean Quarry tile was selected for the vestibule and service areas while Dal-Duraflor was used in the restaurant and the floral departments. The planning center was carpeted. Though the general sales area reflects the price-oriented aspect of the Pick 'N' Save image, the owners, Ron Brash and Lloyd Coopersmith, agreed that the perimeter spaces should be as up-scale as possible. To achieve that desired look, the ceiling along the perimeter was dropped to 10'8″, in contrast to the 16' height in the core grocery area. Also, art deco style

Commercial Interior Products, Tom Huff, C.E.O.
Roundy's Store layout and engineering department
Client: Pick 'N' Save: Lloyd Coopersmith, pres.
Ron Brash, Secretary/Treasurer

graphics were added. To create an outdoors feeling where it counted, the Market Produce and Floral sections were capped with simulated skylight treatments.

Throughout the perimeter shop space, the designers preferred cool, soothing colors. A soffit of sharp teal blue made a fine foil for the white lettering and the space that fills the area between the different ceiling heights was patterned with gray-blue and white tiles in a checkered design.

Lighting was high on the design agenda. To bring emphasis to the product display in the perimeter shops, back-lighted, translucent vinyl fabric awnings were used to filter the light from the fluorescent strips in the ceilings. Above the free standing cases in the deli and other areas, louvers and para-cube lenses were used in the lighting frames. It did require that the light louver be placed directly over the product to work effectively. The high output lamps in the cases added to the overall illumination of the area. In contrast, 400 watt metal halide, warehouse type lighting fixtures were used in the 16' ceiling over the grocery core. They were centered over the aisles rather than the gondolas. Up above, the ceiling was painted a pale teal blue.

Big Y Foods

EAST LONGMEADOW, MA

Design: CDI Designs, Inc., Riverdale, NY

The design concept for this store, which was expanded and remodeled to 42,000 sq. ft., was based solidly on the marketing strategy and target market of the client. East Longmeadow is a community with many shoppers who have minimal time for food preparation, but nevertheless favor fresh foods and are highly nutrition conscious.

It was more than designing a new store. This design concept would be used to unify recently acquired stores and also set a pattern for other neighborhood shopping centers that would be anchored by a Big Y store. Also, the existing store of 25,000 sq. ft. had to be kept open and functioning while the work on the adjacent space was being prepared. When the new work was completed, the operation would then be transferred to the new space while the original store would be refurbished. To achieve Big Y's merchandising goals, perishables and service departments like deli, bakery, and seafood were all expanded around the perimeter of the enlarged space.

Layout and design worked together to achieve ease of shopping and departmental clarity. Specialty departments, identified by a banner signing program, — special lighting, — fixtures, — and custom designed floor tiles, line the perimeters of the store while standard gondola runs carry the basic groceries in the core area of the store. A skylight which begins outside the store as a glass canopy becomes a dramatic focal point in the produce department which extends back from the entrance. Also, banners and lighting combine to feature this key department. See photo on next page.

The bakery (see previous page) has an attractive "soffit" made up of a series of angled canvas cubes composed of banners that carry the signage and add a dramatic brilliance to the otherwise low-keyed, warmly lit area. The hot red contrasts with the icy cool aquas and white of the floor tiles in the frozen food section. Recessed incandescents add their special aura to that of the hidden fluorescents.

Below: A view of the produce area. The floor is gridded with beige bands of tiles that frame the large squares of white. The same neutral beige color is used on the walls and soffits with red making a bright accent ring near the ceiling. The area is predominantly lit with a combination of recessed metal halide lamps in the ceiling and cannister lamps serve to spotlight featured areas of display.

Above: The front end of the produce department with the external skylight becoming a strong element in the decor and the lighting of the space. The sharp red wall (rear) leads into the beige walls that circle the produce department, and the red continues as a pencil line accent. Hanging from the high ceiling over the assembled plants and flowers are aqua banners. In addition to the pendant fixtures, a light trough is suspended over the plants and one also extends out off the red wall. Canopy lights appear over the grocery gondolas and they provide the direct light for this important core area.

The designers also developed a new logo which reflects the client's commitment to quality and service and will also make a Big Y store easy to recognize — and remember. This store won honors in the recent Chain Store Age Executive "Store of the Year" competition for the supermarket remodeling.

Insalaco's Market

HAZELTON, PA

Design: Off-The-Wall, Telford, PA

A warm, intimate sense of space with low-keyed ambient lighting makes the store a friendly place to shop. The color scheme is white with sharp red and grayed blue accents. A red wire grid appears as a unifying design motif throughout the 45,000 sq. ft. of the store. Above, in the grocery area, the grid spans over the self-illuminated, oak finished gondolas and it carries the lighting of products to be found in the particular aisle.

The white tile floor is highlighted with pale blue tiles and bordered with a red insert. In the bakery area, opposite, the red grid is applied over the white soffit and into the arced openings are set white oval signs lettered in red and illuminated by spots recessed in the acoustic tile ceiling. Red lacquered accent pendants hang over the products set against the black and white tiled wall in the rear. In the foreground, feature tables and floor stands are finished in the subtle blue color. The produce area reverses the scheme; white grids frame the red ovals and the floor cases are red tile and natural oak set on blue enameled bases.

The lighting throughout is mainly incandescent with an assist from hidden fluorescent tubes and strip fixtures.

Larry's Market

SEATTLE, WA

Design: Suzi McKinney   Architects: Carlson/Ferrin

When the Seattle chapter of the American Institute of Architects honored the architectural firm of Carlson/Ferrin of Seattle for their prime-winning design for Larry's Market, the jury's comment was: "A project that is exuberant in form and scale without being superficial. It celebrates its shopping center setting, as well as its function through the masterful use of industrial materials. The delightful atmosphere is enhanced by a sophisticated use of color, signage and lighting."

Combine all that with hand painted murals and artwork used instead of traditional signage; — vegetables dancing over the produce area or

SEAFOOD MARKET

'ALWAYS T'

MARKET BUY
$2.59

DEMO TEAM
LEARN HOW TO
CLEAN & PREPARE
SQUID!!

Humpty Dumpty sitting over the eggs, and metal sculptured salmons floating/flying over the seafood section, — add flowers and trees and a 21' ceiling banded with a 5' clerestory for additional light, — and you have an idea what the excitement is all about.

"We wanted to create a happy attitude about food, so we designed the lighting to remind our customers of old-fashioned wholesome freshness. We wanted to create an atmosphere of a big, open air market, so we provided live trees and lots of daylight. "Also, Suzi McKinney, interior designer and wife of Larry McKinney, the owner of Larry's Market, tried to recapture and bring into this large, high-tech structure of 45,000 sq. ft. some of the romance and simple pleasures of the 40s and 50s.

The central part of the store has a raised roof with exposed steel trusses and metal decking. 400 watt metal halide lamps are angled towards the white reflective ceiling, and the light falls on to the highly polished floor made up of diagonal diamonds of celadon green and white. Hunter green and celadon serve as cooling trim colors. There are few interior walls and the exposed food preparation areas make the shoppers feel as though they were in a food store rather than a supermarket.

Larry McKinney describes his store as a "combination warehouse and packing shed" and he "wants customers to really feel they're in a working market." Wanda Adams, writing for a Seattle newspaper shortly after the supermarket opened described it as " — getting past the architecture and checking out the shelves, the impression is that a farmer's market, a bunch of specialty stores and a take-out stand or two collided with a no-frills box store."

Interior Design: Suzi McKinney
Architecture: Donald Carlson & Kevin Kane
of Carlson/Ferrin
Lighting information: Barbara Jo Novitski article
in Architectural Lighting, April '89
Photos: J.P. Housel

Genuardi's

DOYLESTOWN, PA

Design: Off-The-Wall, Telford, PA

Gaspare Genuardi started his business in produce way back in the 1920s when he brought his garden fresh food to his customers on the back of his old truck. Eventually Grandpa Genuardi parked his truck permanently and opened a true "mom and pop" style superette where he, his wife Josephine and their five children all worked. The Genuardi operation is today a 23 store supermarket chain, but still very much a family affair. Their stores are deeply rooted in and are part of the communities they are located in. No matter how large the store gets to be, and this one is 45,000 sq. ft., they always manage to retain a "small town feeling" while merchandising the newest, the best and in the most up-to-date manner.

This store is done predominantly in cool colors with a soft mauve leading the way. The floor is covered with large squares of mauve tile gridded in white, and most of the walls and ceilings are also in mauve. In the Meat area, a cool blue is added to the palette and the walls are covered with decorative ceramic tiles and blue awnings step out over the counters below.

The awnings are used to carry the signage for the specialty shops that line the perimeter of the store and they also shield the customer from the lights behind them that are used to light up the food displayed below.

In order to operate an open market feeling, there are long stretches of vaulted "skylights" that simulate daylight with fluorescent lamps in the plenum above the frosted panes of glass. The cool blues and teals

are used as accents on the mullions. In the produce area, small awnings over the fruits and vegetables suggest the individual stands one finds in the marketplace. Mauve laminates are used to sheath the produce squares out of the floor and also the freezer cabinets.

The graphics and signage are bright and colorful and are reminiscent of the designs of the Pennsylvania Dutch who still live in this area.

Grand Union Food Center

KINGSTON, NY

Design: Milton Glaser Inc., NY

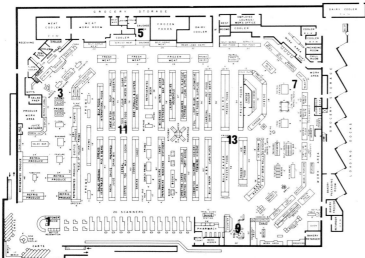

Client: Grand Union
Donald C. Vaillancourt, V.P. of Corp. Communications and Consumer Affairs

In describing the 65,000 sq. ft. supermarket that opened up 100 miles north of NYC, Warren Thayer, writing in Progressive Grocer (Sept. '88) called it "Grand Union's Grandest." This is a store that seems embarked on being and having something for everyone. Frank J. Breen, Sr., one of the operational V.P.s of Grand Union said, "we focus our attention not so much on demographics as in the service/ quality niche that can appeal to both a $200 a week mill worker and a $2,000 a week executive." With this wide view of target in mind, it is delightful to see a store devoid of splashy paper signs closing up all the windows, but once inside the familiar red dot specials quickly point the way to the super specials.

The color scheme is simple and un-complicated. It has been reduced to light gray and mauve tiled floors,

with white tiled walls and lots and lots of sparkling red accents. There are red tiles set into the white tiled walls, — red bands streamline the white enameled cases and counters, and red enameled metal shades hold the incandescent lamps that are directed down at the food products. Even the grocery carts get into the act — or design scheme — and the red metal mesh carriers sit on chromed chassis. Left: The sausage kitchen gets a "homey" touch with light wood paneling outlined with red around the windows. The sign is a red plaque with white lettering.

Clustered together near the rear end of the store, set cater-corner to attract the traffic, is the seafood area. Up front is a refrigerated seafood

cabinet with a promotional table in front of it. Chowders and condiments flank it. Behind is the display of fresh fish (see below) as well as a fish-fry set up and a service counter. Beyond, and open for viewing are the work tables, coolers and freezers. The soffit is natural wood, banded in red. The green glass shades are combined with fluorescent luminaires to provide bright ambient and clear accent lighting. The cases and counters are also accented with red and natural wood, and lengths of wood are stretched over the white tiled walls as decorative band.

There are all sorts of prepared goods available at Grand Union, — to take home or snack on in the store. Upper right: One of the service bars where smart red and white signs clearly indicate what is available and also provides informa-

tion about the ingredients, quantities and prices. In this area the pendant shades are red and just about everything is red and white. Below right: Is the very popular "Make Your Own Taco" bar. It is set out on the aisle not too far from the tantilizing smell and sizzle of the freshly made pizza, — or for those who prefer — frozen ones to take home to finish. Also at this end of the store is the bakery where the shopper can buy bread, bagels, popcorn, muffins, cakes and pastries — or even get a special occasion cake trimmed and inscribed while you wait.

On its 47,261 sq. ft. of space, this store seems to have something for everyone. There is a sense or excitement and dynamic action in the store; the colors are sharp and fresh, the lighting is bright yet easy on the eye and flattering to the products.

The signage is easy to find — simple to follow, and if it is raining when you are ready to leave with your fully packed red cart, there are giant red and white Grand Union umbrellas conveniently located near the exits that the shopper may borrow.

Yaohan Supermarket

WATERSIDE PLAZA, EDGEWATER, NJ

Design: Ecoplan, Englewood Cliffs, NJ

The interior design of the super-market, especially the Food Court, is unique in an American market. At Yaohan, the small food concessions provide a variety of ethnic foods, — Japanese, Chinese, Italian and American — in a plan that is reminiscent of an outdoor carnival or bazaar with a central eating station utilized by all the vendors. The 49,250 sq. ft. supermarket is not only the largest, but it is the most complete Japanese supermarket in the U.S. The exterior design has a stucco like finish and is banded with green and an heroic grid of the green completes one end of the rectangular facade. Red awnings add a cheery note over the small retail shops.

Metal halide and fluorescent fixtures light up the bright, white interior and everywhere there are accents of red. Handsome materials

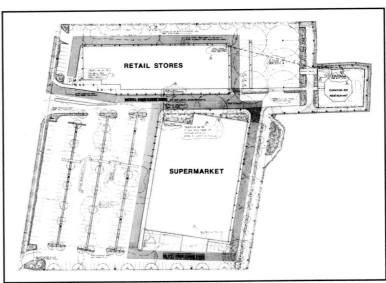

Client: Yaohan Dept. Stores, Co. Ltd., Japan
Yaohan, U.S.A., Edgewater, NJ
Developer: Feldman Enterprises, Hackensack, NJ
Photos: Jay Rosenblatt / Scott McKiernan

are used throughout and the refinement of the design is apparent as one enters under a canopy of skylights that echo the peaked entrance into the market. Design elements that are uniquely Japanese are incorporated into the otherwise contemporary scheme to reinforce the fact that this is the seventh Yaohan Supermarket in the United States operated by the Yaohan

Department Store Co. Ltd. in Japan. On the previous page, the short red and white curtain that serves as a canopy over the display of Promotional goods is typical of the hanging fabric panels in front of shops in Japan. In the produce area, below, the natural wood beam constructions bound with rope are also traditional in design and in concept. The red/white akari lanterns provide a

festive and colorful accent to the
beamed elements that dramatically
highlight the whole area.

The entire Food Court theme,
above, is unified by the use of mirror finish stainless steel trim and
decorative neon used for signage
and ornamentation. The spectacular
octagonal fixture that swoops down
through the octagonal dropped ceiling lights up the wood floor and the
white tables and chairs. At Yaohan
Plaza, — West meets East — and
likes it.

Asda

KENT, ENGLAND

Design: Fitch & Co., London

When the growing Asda chain, which was based predominantly in the North of England, wanted to "up-market" (up-scale their image) and also establish themselves in the more affluent south of England, they called upon the Fitch Company to create a new identity and trading format. The result is a very contemporary store which incorporates bold graphics, and is suffused with green to suggest Asda's emphasis on freshness of product. The green is applied freely on the fascias, — on the signs, and the packaging.

The exterior facade is bright and colorful in yellow, green and aqua with accents of other primaries. The shopper enters and then descends to the below ground, 50,000 sq. ft. store and is welcomed by a high vaulted ceiling washed with light. The main sources of light for this big, open, white area are the metal halide lamps and fluorescents. Fitch & Co. created specialized areas for the bakery (lower right), the fish shop and the delicatessen, and with the greater emphasis on freshness and quality, they improved the presentation of vegetables and fruits. In addition, distinct identities were created for Sound & Vision, the Spirits section (upper right) and other non-food departments. The emphasis on green in the graphics, signage and decor is effectively shown in the Wine and Liquor area.

Von's Pavilions

ARCADIA, CA

Design: McClellan Cruz Gaylord & Assoc.

This 50,000 sq. ft. store is the major tenant in a 200,000 sq. ft. community shopping center. The exterior of the supermarket, in Von's tradition, is concrete block covered with white stucco and then accented with an elaborate white spaceframe over the entrance. Superimposed over the lace-work of metal rods is a "Pavilions" sign in red with the double "V" logo beneath it that is readable from out on the highway. Inside, the store is also all gleaming white floors, walls, cases and ceiling. The large space looms even larger in its pristine whiteness.

The colorful canvas swags that are

used as signage and as decor make bright impressions against all the white. Here, in the deli area, the red and violet combine for shock and startle. Smaller signs, also in red with white lettering, are used as subheadings, or to explain the individual offerings under the main area captions.

A center island, shown below, features a mini-deli and a baked goods area. Since there are almost no interior walls, all the preparation work is done out in full view of the shoppers as is the food arranging, and the meat cutting and slicing. Shoppers can stop and snack on the fresh goodies they have just pur-

chased. Stools and a table surface are conveniently located in the middle of all the smells and sights.

HID lamps are recessed into the ceiling, but spotlights are plentiful and they add a warm, rich color to the collected foodstuffs below. White tubular canopies, with fluorescent tubes embedded, are dropped over counters and special presentation squares. In addition, the lighting plan also calls for pendant incandescent fixtures which flood selected areas with warm light.

The bright red of the canvas swags and banners and the signs is also us-

ed as accent strips on the white walls, — as enameled trim on the cases, cabinets and railings, and also for drop cloths on feature tables. Natural oak is incorporated into the red and white scheme for a homey quality.

Above: A closer look at the snack counter in the Deli area, and a view

146

of the assorted light sources that are combined in the total light plan.

In some areas of the store, high stock shelving is employed. It is similar to those used in popular warehouse stores and it is used for impact and to suggest special values. Live lobsters swim about in tanks in the Fish market, butchers will prepare special cuts in the Meat shop, the customer can have a freshly made ice cream cone, enjoy assorted ethnic delicacies or the shopper can bring home a bottle of wine from the Wine Cellar and fresh flowers from the Floral shop for dinner. For the unexpected headache, there are aspirin, and many other things, available at the Pharmacy. Truly, it is "variety and convenience in one-stop at Von's Pavilions."

Developing Designs for Supermarkets

To be a big fish in a small pond or small fish in the sea? Years ago, that according to my mother was my most important career decision. Traipsing off to New York and dressing like Doris Day, (now you know just how many years ago) was the only career decision as far as I was concerned. It was the furthest thought in my mind to end up designing supermarkets.

Only a decade or two ago, supermarkets were garishly lighted, over crowded boxes with high ceilings and cardboard bananas strung all over the place. The concept of customer shopping comfort was not yet conceived. For an interior designer, this added up to less than fertile career potential. Today, this has all changed, and changed with a vengeance. Not only are supermarkets becoming first class retail citizens, they are doing so at a fast pace.

In the past, professional design firms were not interested in the supermarket arena. Store decor was just another commodity which was purchased a couple of months before the store opened. The only designing necessary was to make sure that wall letters or styrofoam graphics would indeed fit in the spaces available.

The picture changed when a few important occurrences came together in a relatively short period of time. First, the computer entered the picture. Today's supermarkets are outstripping even the most sophisticated department stores in their use of this time saving tool.

Second, wholesalers and cooperatives became stronger, and began to offer many services previously done on an individual basis by store owners.

Third, a second generation came into the business. This was a generation to whom the industry and the basics with which their parents had struggled, was second nature. They were up and running, with a track record to guide them. They knew the trends and they had their fingers on the pulse of the ever changing consumer. A consumer who was beginning to demand more; in prepared foods, in convenience, in services. When owners began worrying about how to meet the needs of a time pressed two career family, they entered the realm of customer psychology. Along with that came a sensitivity to other non tangible aspects of "super-marketing," one of these being customer comfort as it relates to the shopping environment.

Lighting is one of the key elements. In 1979 I received my illumination certification from the Illumination Engineering Society of North America. From 1979 until 1984 I expounded the principles of good lighting in supermarkets, and no one was interested. Open strip lighting was it. After a few years, I got a few nibbles on the subject and a few takers. Today however, there is not a supermarket we design where the owner does not designate good lighting as a top design priority. A few short years from strip lights to spot lights, and what a difference.

Good design is a marriage of many disciplines from the knowledge of materials to lighting. Specifically, in a supermarket you have reflected ceiling plans, lighting, flooring, casework, and graphics. To offer all of these design services takes a staff of different people, mainly because design schools divide curriculum into separate specialties. Designers who are proficient in graphics and signing generally are not trained in the functions of interior design. The drafting that is required to communicate the information to the contractors building a store is another discipline altogether. A design firm offering all of these services employs a number of people, each with special training.

Developments have happened in every other area of supermarket design, and this keeps the business exciting. It is exciting because it is no longer complacent. It is constantly moving, changing, and stimulating. Most of all, the owners are enthusiastic. They want good design, and they demand good design. Remodeling a sad looking market into a beautiful shopping environment or creating an exciting new store, ground up, has enormous emotional rewards.

Barbra G. Barker, President
Off The Company, Inc.

148

Chapter Four

50,000
To
100,000
Square Feet

Super Shaw's

DERRY, NH

Design: CDI Designs Inc., Riverdale, NY

This design represents the second generation of Super Shaw stores — a more cohesive and integrated design for the 52,000 sq. ft., full line supermarket with a core section of massed grocery displayed on warehouse shelving plus a variety of high quality service departments. In this up-dated version, the lighting is designed to enhance the merchandise presentation while still maintaining strict standards of energy efficiency. Graphics, wall treatments, floor tile designs, ceiling heights, and other design elements are coordinated to define departments and project a unique Shaw identity. Graphics and department identification feature American Typewriter type face set at a 17.5 degree angle.

The same graphic is carried through

in a completely controlled range of signage, — from directory information to price signage to promotional and vendor signage. By this strict adherence to a single "style" of graphic type, the visual clutter that often appears in overlaid miscellaneous and vendor signage is eliminated.

The all white interiors are high-lighted, predominantly, with red and green on the signs, on the HVAC pipes, and the canvas awnings that not only lower the ceilings over special feature stands, but also serves as bold signage panels. Above, the red awning picks out the Deli and further back, the baked goods are displayed under a mari-gold colored, sawtooth arrangement of canvas panels.

World Class Shop Rite

BETHLEHEM SQ., BETHLEHEM, PA
Design: Off-The-Wall, Telford, PA

Since Foodarama Shop Rite's management wanted their new 55,000 sq. ft. store to be "the most beautiful in the chain," and they were willing to pay for it, the designers considered an architectural approach to the design rather than one dependent upon surface decoration. Elaborate multiple stepped drops were planned to lower ceilings in some areas, and to vault ceilings in others, — thus taking the shopper from one special environment to another. The appropriate heights were determined by the particular lighting needs of each area's merchandise.

The selection of a dark grocery area ceiling was made to

create the effect of causing the ceiling drops to advance and the ceiling to recede. "In this store, the desire was to have the structure itself, not the color of the structure, be a major design element. A strict adherence to the selected color palette and the exclusive use of a single major design element creates a total unified look."

Non-glare lighting was used throughout, and the designers have been awarded the Edwin F. Guth Memorial Award for Lighting from the Illumination Engineering Society of North America for their work on this store.

Bel Air Market

CARMICHAEL, CA

Design: King Design, Eugene, OR

Client: Bel Air Markets
Geroge Wong, President
Bill Wong, Director of Produce

There has been a long marriage between client and designer, and over the many happy years of working together various design concepts and interior layouts have evolved, — along with the owner's own philosophy of merchandising. Bel Air Markets is a well established, family-owned, supermarket chain. The motto is "The Stores that Care," and the management gives the customers every opportunity to become involved, — and the management listens. The current design, shown here in this 55,000 sq. ft. store, establishes a warm, clean and friendly feeling.

The overall utilization of large photo murals creates a recognizable image for customers. Neon signage is added for additional information and for the highlighting it provides. The reflective color also adds to the murals. The color palette for the interior is warm and filled with earthy colors starting with an off-white on the floor and toning up to peach/beige on the walls with accents and soffit designs in golds, oranges, red-orange, sienna and brown. Lots of rich oak is used for trimming and framing the floor fixtures and the striped and banded soffits. Assorted color canvas awnings hang over the specialty shops that follow the perimeter walls of the market. The awnings range from blue in the seafood section, to red in gourmet meats over to cheese where the awning is orange. The checkerboard design on the back wall of the service space is color keyed to the awning up front. Crystal pendant fixtures hang directly over the products displayed in the oak-trimmed cases. Fluorescent strips light up the service area and the fixtures are contained within the awnings. Out on the floor tubular metal frames, with fluorescent lamps embedded, are used as lighting rectangles over the island cases and stands.

Brown's Super Shop Rite

SNYDER PLAZA, PHILADELPHIA, PA

Design: Off-The-Wall, Telford, PA

The client said, "Contemporary — like a spaceship." The designers would have opted for a red, green and white color scheme that they thought would be more in keeping for a 55,000 sq. ft. store in a densely populated area that is predominantly Italian in heritage. However, the success of the client's instincts were not to be argued with.

Instead, warm dark colors were selected with copper and brass touches and accents of pink and turquoise neon. The soft toned ceilings were lowered over the perimeter service departments, and totally glare-free lighting fixtures were specified. Translucent awnings, which were back lighted — for a glowing effect, and black plexiglas panels created a high-tech ceiling and graphic focal points. Low ambience light levels contrast with the dramatic, high merchandise illumination. To balance the dynamic high tech quality of the design, a handsome serif type was selected for all the signage.

The contemporary feeling is set, up front, at the checkouts. The predominant color is mauve, — from the light tints mixed on the floor, — painted on the ceiling, to the deeper shade for the blinds that fill the front window expanse. A black metal grid is played against the graphic grid of white on black used on the overhead signs in the mauve lacquered "arrows." A cool blue stripe is used as an accent.

The assorted mauves in the tiled floor make a light looking base for the sleek black freezer cases that are lined up under a dropped ceiling of copper colored baffles. The multi-angled soffit is finished in

mauve and black with a pink neon stripe for sizzle. A streamlining band of black plexiglas runs over the wall freezers and carries the elegant signage.

The butcher shop is a butcher shop. Ribbed crystal pendants hang down over the prepared packages of meat, and directly behind the low black and chrome cases is the actual preparation area with butchers in attendance. Note the back-lit, translucent awning that accentuates this shop's location under the dropped ceiling. The same sophisticated looks is maintained in the grocery area located opposite the frozen foods section previously mentioned. The overhead, identifying signs are black with white, and accented with the cool blue. The gondolas are finished in black and each has a projecting black canopy on top to shield the shopper from the fluorescent tubes that are illuminating the products on display below.

Albertson's

SLIDELL, LA

Design: Albertson's Store Design Group

Architect of Record-Interior: Henricks-Callaway
Architect of Record-Exterior: DPF Architects
Exterior Photo: Marcus Lamkin
Interior Photo: Dennis Thurston, Albertson's

It has been fifty years since Joe Albertson opened his first grocery store in Boise, Idaho. The business covered approximately 10,000 sq. ft. and employed thirty people, — and made a profit of nearly $10,000 in the first year. Over the passing years, Albertson's has expanded throughout the northwest and today the chain consists of almost five hundred stores in seventeen western and southern states with nine distribution facilities. The growth and success is attributed to Joe Albertson's very practical philosophy, "We have always had full confidence that if we give the customers the kind of merchandise they want at a price they can afford to pay, and maintain clean stores with friendly personnel, — we can't help but be successful."

In Albertson's, produce areas have rapidly expanded to meet the growing needs of the health-conscious consumer. Under a ceiling filled with bright fluorescent strip fixtures, on a mottled gray/ white vinyl floor, there is an explosion of color and a mass display of produce. The store's emphasis on freshness and quality is reinforced in the presentation. Bushel baskets serve as "supports" for the bounty of fruits above. The baskets plus the cardboard cartons suggest "just in" and "just unpacked," and what could be fresher than that. In keeping with the produce, the soffit is diagonally patterned in shades of green with simple block letters in green.

Also, — for the health-oriented and

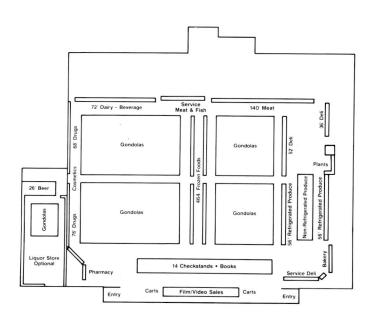

those in a hurry, a salad bar has become a standard fixture in an Albertson's store. In some stores, the signage is more folksy and recommends savings.

Albertson's finds that the combination Foods & Drugs unit is the most exciting store format. It is part of the one-stop shopping concept that they have pioneered. These combination units meet the needs of customers who desire to buy more than food on a typical shopping trip. This store of 59,000 sq. ft. carries over 40,000 different items.

In one of the specialty areas, Plants & Flowers, just beyond the produce

area: natural wood strips line the soffit and the applied lettering stands away with a matching frame around the letters. Beneath the soffit, rows of fluorescent strips are covered by a frosted plastic panel, and they create a bright daylight effect. The floor is the same textured off-white vinyl that covers the floors throughout the store.

Each year Albertson's remodels thirty to forty stores in order to keep them attractive — and competitive. "Albertson's is a big store with a specialty store approach. We must be 'big' in terms of low prices, convenience and wide selection of brands. We must be a 'specialty store' in terms of quality, personal service and specialized selection."

Dillons

OLATHE, KS

Design: Dillons' Store Planning Group

"Much of the company's dynamic growth (is attributed) to a combination of independent, operator-style, friendliness, customer services, shiny clean stores, quality products and our innovative spirit," wrote Lee Dyer in an article that appeared in Progressive Grocer. This mega-operation, that has been servicing the food needs of Kansans for almost 70 years, has a "penchant for trying new approaches," and this 60,000 sq. ft. super store is one of the company's newest approaches to store design and layout.

Olathe is a suburb of Kansas City and is a town of rapid growth and development. One of the new features introduced in this store is the self-service sandwich and taco bar that is located up front in the highly trafficked area near the entrance to produce. It is an expansion of the full-service deli area which Dillons introduced into their stores in the 70s. Placing the sandwich bar next to the salad bar was an inspired move since one complemented the other, and together they created a great focal point for shoppers ready for a quick snack.

The light colored, shiny floor has become a signature note in a Dillons design. The pale speckled floor is highlighted with a wide band of color. This store is done in a palette of warm earth tones with the soft beige and natural oak wood holding the accent colors together. In the deli area, (upper left) the warm brown color that bands the floor is complemented by the sienna colored canvas awning that serves as a fascia facade for this specialty area. The canopy not only shields the shopper from the fluorescent strip lights behind the

canopy, it also carries the departmental signage. The 32-foot long, European styled cases in the deli area are also specially detailed with ceramic tiles, on the base, in a pattern of beige and terra cotta. Two feet out from the cases, recessed in the dropped ceiling, are long rows of fluorescent luminaires that brighten up the space.

The cases in the seafood section (lower left) have ceramic tile bases done in pale green and beige. A deeper green sign carries the department signage in white. The soffit that bands this area is embellished with photomurals of seafood. These two shops are only part of the array of service shops that line the rear perimeter of the store.

The produce section (above) is trimmed with a soft avocado green accented with brown, and natural wood is tastefully applied as mold-

ings, frames for the graphics, and occasional panels, — all to enhance the "natural" and "homey" aspects of the design. Large photographics decorate the wood soffit in this well illuminated area.

One of the big draws at Dillons is the pizza stand which sells freshly made pizzas, prepared and baked on the floor, which appears as an adjunct to the cheese shop. The cheese island is rendered in orange and gold tones from the enameled refrigerated cases up to the large glass shades with incandescent lamps that hang off the wood lattice framework that distinguishes this area. The warmth of Dillons comes not only from the beiges, golds, oranges, siennas, browns and greens of the decor, — it comes from the smiling, service-oriented salespersons and the customer-involved layout and displays of the store.

Advantage Supermarket

SAN DIEGO, CA

Design: Addison Design Consultants, San Francisco, CA

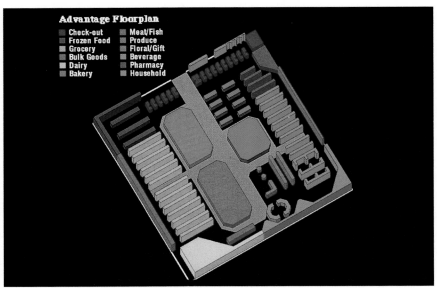

Advantage Floorplan

- Check-out
- Frozen Food
- Grocery
- Bulk Goods
- Dairy
- Bakery
- Meat/Fish
- Produce
- Floral/Gift
- Beverage
- Pharmacy
- Household

Chain Store Age recently selected Advantage as the "new store of the year," and saluted it as a consumer focused supermarket. They called it a store that "was designed for people who hate to shop" and they describe it as "open, uncluttered and functional." The 60,000 sq. ft. store was targeted towards the price sensitive shopper with a limited amount of time. The airy, contemporary store provides an unobstructed vista for shoppers entering at the front door. Checkout registers are heralded by bright horizontal signs hung from a white spaceframe, and they flank the

Client: Lucky Stores, Inc.
Lighting Design: CDI, NY
Specialty Fixtures and Displayers: Newood Products

front doors. The 20 ft. wide center aisle is banded with colored vinyl tiles that make a pattern to follow. On the main aisle the shopper passes by special food islands, — fresh produce on crates for discerning shoppers, — a fresh fish and meat department with butchers in attendance, — a deli with a full time chef, and a bakery with desserts and pastries made on the premises. The primary and secondary drive aisle systems make it simple for the shopper to find what she wants.

Vertical banners are color coded in happy primary colors and they serve

to delineate and identify areas and the products contained. In addition, white awnings crown the specialty shops and areas on the open floor and provide a more intimate sense of space in this large, high ceilinged operation. The awnings are banded in red and the signage in white. Supported from the awning are pendant incandescent fixtures that add a glow to the foods beneath.

Where the groceries are stacked, the gondolas are illuminated by a

ceiling grid that hangs above them. Lengths of fluorescent strips appear between the gondolas. A decorative fascia runs along the aisle identifying the products behind. The overall lighting for the open space is provided by HID lamps. The diamond pattern of white and gray floor tiles serves as a border around the free standing shops and also is a directional force on the main, wide aisle.

The store's layout differs from the more common race-track configura-tion usually found in grocery stores. Most items are clustered and located in a way which allows customers to shop only in specific areas fulfilling their needs. Frozen Foods are strategically located near the checkout lanes as the last area to shop, the product adjacencies are also well planned.

The salad bar is only one of the special features in this store and it does make a pleasant stop in the long run of the central aisle.

Loblaws Garden Market

TORONTO, ONT., CANADA

Design: The Watt Group, Toronto, Ont., Canada

The Garden Market Center is located in a suburb of Toronto and in 62,000 sq. ft. it combines a supermarket with a garden center. This operation is the latest in a series of Watt Group designs for the Loblaw Company. Over the 15 or more years of design association Lowlaw's has been "repositioned from an ailing chain to a market leader through strategic store design and communication programs."

"The Watt Group understands that the product is the package, and that the key to communicating a

business's or product's unique pro-position to the consumer is visibility — increasingly difficult to achieve amid the clutter of competing messages within the growing scale of new retail environments. We develop business solutions using design as a tool, — creating cor-porate identity and packaging which responds to the scale of retail space, and packaging retail en-vironments with an implicit understanding of visual communica-tions."

At Loblaw's the design is focused on product presentation and clear direct signage. Giant photomurals suspended from metal overhead grids provide direction and informa-tion for the shopper. They tell her where what is located and because they are high up, the colorful pro-duct photos are readily viewed from most parts of the store. Up close, where the merchandise is located, the signs are simple, clear and co-ordinated. The Red/Green color note sounded on the facade con-tinues on the interior. The signs are green with white lettering while the metal grids that support the graphics and other large signs are painted red. In produce, green enameled spot housings add a touch of color, while in meat, the red housings on the red tracks go with the metal framework. The in-teriors are clean, uncluttered and well lit, and the "visual communica-tion" is on target.

Kroger
FOREST HILLS, CINCINNATI, OH
Design: Hixson Inc., Cincinnati, OH

Kroger's is proud that it "responds to today's lifestyles," and this store is an example of one that is lifestyle-oriented in its merchandise — its operation and its strategies. Each of the many Kroger stores is designed to respond to the changing consumer needs and the competitive environment, and also reflect, area by area, the wide variety of shoppers' tastes and preferences, and still bring the shoppers what they want.

The red brick exterior facade is broken with gables and highlighted with green and white striped awnings. A clock tower dominates one end of the structure and with the arched openings at the base, it adds a traditional quality to an otherwise contemporary building.

Inside the 70,000 sq. ft. store, the overall lighting is low-keyed, — subdued, pleasant and relaxing. The fluorescents are recessed in the not overly high ceiling, and the neon signage on the perimeter soffits sings out in the low light.

Client: The Kroger Company
Architect/Engineer: Hixson Inc.
Paul Frey, R.A. Project Manager
Store Planning: The Kroger Co./Hixson Inc./
Retail Planning Associates
Photos: Cam-Tech, Dick Loesch

The taupe/gray vinyl floors are highly polished and the main aisle is white vinyl and is gridded and bordered with red vinyl strips. The cases and counters are white enamel trimmed with red, and in the refined, quiet light, — the red neon signs make a visual impact and then a decorative "puddle" on the reflective floors. Hidden ceiling washers cast a halo of light where the soffit and ceiling meet. The cafe was designed in taupe and white with natural oak which is used to provide a warm, traditional ambience. The ribbed pendant lamps cast a warm light over each table and the prepared foods are illuminated by the fluorescents hidden under the soffit over the serving counter.

Below: A long view of the produce area. The ceilings throughout this store are about 12 feet high and have long runs of fluorescent luminaires with soft diffusing lenses. The individual selling areas are tiled in taupe/gray vinyl off the red gridded white aisles bordered in red. The grocery gondolas, seen beyond the produce, are low in profile and a dropped light canopy over the gondola brings the light down to the product. A juice bar is centrally located between the produce area and the specialty shops that follow the perimeter walls of the selling space. In this full view one can see how effective the white and red neon signs are when set against the warm gray soffit.

With Kroger's approach to making each store suit its location, — being tailor made to its special market — to its customers' taste-level and lifestyle, we can see the low-keyed, relaxed, upscaled shopper ambling along the generous aisles finding the products he/she expects to find — at a competitive price.

Rouse's

HOUMA, LA

Design: Architectonics, Huntington Sta., NY

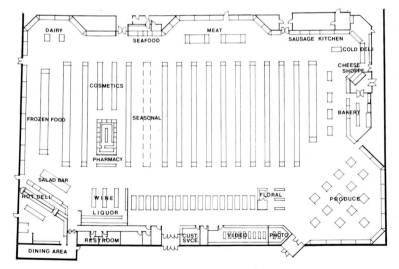

"The design challenge was to not overwhelm the customer with the vast space (70,000 sq. ft.). Order and definition were key considerations for the successful presentation of so much diverse merchandise." The client did want to capture a large audience and attract a new and different clientele, and in a "modern,

open, clean-lined store" maintain the price conscious image. The shopper enters into Rouse's Garden, an impactful space — 120' deep, with simulated skylights above. The floors and ceiling are white, and the green of the walls is used to grid the floor. The orange of the supergraphic letters reappears on the cases that line the perimeter. On the floor, natural wood "crates" serve as feature tables for the fresh produce.

In Frozen Foods, the color scheme switches to blue and white for both the graphic signage and the flooring, while in the meat area red takes over. The use of bold geometric shapes for the architecture, fixtures and flooring color coded by department, are "married together to create order out of potential chaos and individual worlds are developed by shape, color and material."

Baker's

DEERFIELD PLASE CENTER, OMAHA, NE

Design: Peterson Associates, Hinsdale, IL

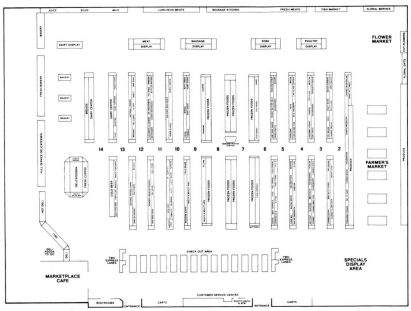

"Quality selection and undeniably small-town friendly service are not only part of their name, but part of the experience of shopping Baker's," says Ted Peterson of Peterson Associates, "and unique product strategies and customer excitement are the foundation for this store's shopping experience." The big time and big city excitement have come to Omaha with the construction of this 73,000 sq. ft. new concept store that offers specialties, gourmet-to-go prepared foods, a full service Market Place Cafe for breakfast, lunch or dinner, a scratch bakery, complete fish service and more than 30,000 products to choose from. Also in this return trip is "a resurgence in the lost art of personal, customer-driven service."

The shopper is invited to watch foods being prepared, meat being sliced, cut and packaged, fish fileted and festive occasion cakes

---

Peterson Associates: Ted Peterson, President
Michael Ferguson, Dir. Facilities Planning
Marshall S. Bohlin, Dir. Graphic Communications
Bahr, Vermeer & Haecker Architects, Omaha
Paul C. Jeffery, Architect
Photos: Mike Whye, Council Bluff

being trimmed. Everywhere there is action and theater in the full round. Of the ten stores in the Baker chain, this is not only the largest but the most stimulating.

The floors are gleaming white as are the cases, the counters, and the walls in the service areas. Stretching across the store, overhead and set

well below the exposed metal trusses, pipes and supports, is a great white metal grid that tends to bring the store down to a more human-scaled height. Hanging from the grid are heroic-sized banners in bright red with white lettering that identify departments in the store and supply some graphic excitement to the controlled interior. White banners alternate with the

red. 400 watt HID lamps provide crisp, clear light on the selling floor.

"The image of this store is no different from our other stores," says Jack Baker, president of Bakers. "We feel that the store has everything to appeal to customers in all income groups. It is not strictly up-scale, although there are up-scale departments and products. It's a store developed to appeal to all customers regardless of their age, income group or household status." There is a difference! The store combines a marketplace atmo-

sphere with small specialty shops, and spacious wide aisles lead to small, intimate spaces. The shopper enters facing the 18 mauve tinted counters touched with red. Red horizontal banners hang over the run of checkout counters and bring the ceiling height down over this area. "We were trying to achieve a contemporary timeless look," says Mr. Baker, "so we employed white as the primary color with feature colors of red and green."

With all food preparation done in full view of the shoppers, it is not only "theater," it shows the freshness and "just made" quality of the food and also makes evident the cleanliness surrounding the handling and preparation of the foods. The central core of the store is devoted to runs of gondolas with dry goods and groceries. In the middle of the floor are two major aisles with low and high freezer cases and a Micro Wave Cooking Center located right in the middle of the area — and the store. Across the rear end of the store are free standing cases as well as perimeter wall cases for poultry, pork, sausages and meat. The Sausage Factory and the Fish Market, complete with tanks of live fish and lobsters, are also located at this end of the store. On the left side of the store, heading back towards the entrance the shopper passes the dairy section and the bakery. Adjacent to the 32' long self-service cheese case, that stands in the aisle, is a 24' U-shaped salad bar that is one of the most popular places in the store. The Coffee Bean Corner provides the shopper with a place to sample a cup of freshly brewed coffee while making a selection from a wide assortment of beans that are ground to order. The deli area is big and important. 49 feet of European-style, refrigerated cases carry a vast selection of prepared foods. In addition there are hot cases for those foods that need to be kept warm.

Back at the front of the store is the Market Place Cafe which can seat almost 170 persons and serves breakfast, lunch and dinner. "Specials Up Front" is located up front, between the checkout counters and the produce area on the right. 5000 sq. ft. of prime space is devoted to the "specials" that are available in the store.

This Baker's is really big news to the shoppers in Omaha.

185

Dominick's Food & Drug

WILLOWBROOK, IL

Design: Dominick's Store Planning Department

Design: Louis Germano, Dominick's Store Planning
Lighting: Juno/Holophone/Crescent
Decor: Programmed Products
Client: Dominick's Finer Food, Northlake, IL

"To keep abreast of ever-changing conditions in this highly competitive food market, — one which is growing more competitive each day, Dominick's Finer Food stores are constantly being remodeled, modernized and improved." This new store of 76,000 sq. ft. represents the latest concept for a Dominick Food and Drug combo store. The design goal was to reinforce Dominick's reputation for quality, selection and service, and special emphasis was given to each perishable or service department.

Large photo murals, accent lighting, up-grade finishes and colorful banners signal the shopper to come to where they can expect personalized service. Unique fixturing and specialized lighting techniques were employed to bring special emphasis to the merchandise. "All of these specialized areas reside within a vast neutral variety of selection offered to the consumer." Wide aisles and a simple traffic pattern

make the store easy to shop.

In addition to the industrial size metal halide lamps used in the corrugated ceiling above, white enameled ceiling tracks outline the areas set out on the white vinyl floor. Above, in the bulk food area where the barrels suggest volume and good prices, the incandescent spots warm up the space with peach light. Over the electrified rectangles

are large mounted photo-murals that serve as signage and they are viewable throughout the store.

Ethnic foods get a stylish presentation between the black ceiling grid, over the gondolas, and the shiny black floor off the white aisle. Here, too, incandescents highlight the signage and the shelved products and the lamps are attached to the dropped grid.

Omni Superstore

ORLAND PARK, IL

Design: Schafer Associates, Oakbrook Terrace, IL
Louis Germano, Dir. of Store Planning, Dominicks

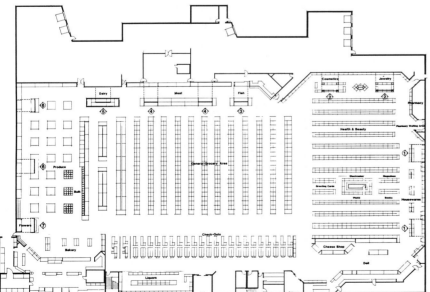

Decor: Programmed Products
Lighting: Juno/Lithania/Holophane
Fixtures: Lozier/Tyler Refrig.
Client: Dominick's Finer Foods, Northlake, IL

"The Omni Superstore was conceived to provide the customer with exceptional quality and freshness of food plus a full variety of food and non-food at the lowest possible prices. As such, the design intent was to create an environment that would differentiate the Omni from both full service supermarkets and bare-bone, warehouse stores. It was considered vital that the Omni be perceived as offering both higher quality and greater variety than any competitive food/combo/warehouse store in the marketplace."

To communicate both the highest quality in perishables and general merchandise, and the lowest possible discount pricing within a single retail concept, the designers evolved a simple, austere shell which was characterized by exposed construction, uniform HID lighting and supergraphics. Introduced within that space was highly individualized specialty departments. Each specialty shop is differentiated by a stylized "shop front," a unique logo, and accent lighting. The "store-within-a-store" concept was to stress that Omni is a one-stop shopping experience.

The color scheme, like the structure, is simple — but dynamic. The black and white provide sheer, sharp contrasts and the red is an emphatic, attention-riveting accent. The wide aisles and open floors are covered with white tiles, and colored diamonds of red and black

create patterns on the floor, — provide a sense of direction, — and are also used to suggest a unique quality for specialty areas. See the Great Lakes Seafood shop on the bottom of the previous page. Between the high-tech ceiling above and the gleaming white floor is a striking black soffit that wraps around the perimeter walls and serves to lower the ceilings over the specialty shops that hug the walls. Super scaled photo murals are applied to the unifying black band. Space frames of white metal tubing and special metal canopies span the aisles or sit over featured products on the floor cases or stands. On the previous page note the overhead arcade that

joins the perimeter shop with the auxiliary and related items on the floor and emphasizes the importance of Hero's Deli department.

The Cosmetic/Jewelry area, above, is highlighted and softened by the addition of the pink superstructure over the light gray cases and counters.

The 86,000 sq. ft. store also includes a pharmacy, a camera and film shop, a video center, a Home-town housewares and hardware area, and more. This is truly a super store — and an auspicious first entry in super-warehouse retailing.

Supermarkets: Looking to the 90's

It seems that every time one views the business section of the newspaper another supermarket chain has either expanded, acquired, or merged with another chain. In 1988, six major merger and acquisition deals, worth $5.8 billion, had been consummated.

Concurrent to these transactions, some chains focused some of their advertising campaign on their independence and many "hypermarkets" — stores of over 200,000 square feet — came onto the scene. The competition for the consumer's attention is more than heated, it is ruthless.

In order to establish their individual identity and image, there is perhaps no other single element more important than the architectural design of the building. Supermarket design has long been an aesthetic challenge for even the most innovative of designers. The building must be distinct yet blend in compatibly with the residential neighborhood. It must convey a sense of quality and stability but be frugal and spartan in design image. In short, although in many respects a large supermarket is simply a warehouse of food, an atmosphere of comfort must be created to lend to a pleasant shopping experience.

To accomplish this, the designs of the 90's will focus on projecting an all-inclusive shopping center on the exterior design. The supermarket is more than a food store. It is a pharmacy, deli, hot bakery, soft goods store, coffee shop, liquor store, salad bar, stationery and hardware store. At the "market" you can order video movies, glasses, cameras and other non-food merchandise. The exterior design of the buildings must convey this multi-faceted ability. Emphasis will not be on form but on volume. Simple materials such as concrete block will continue to be the material of aesthetic and economic choice, but more fanciful graphics, light colors and innovative entrance canopy designs will be called upon to mitigate the warehouse image and fulfill the obligatory individual identity challenge.

Internal store planning will concentrate on creating departments that help to environmentally condense the large expanse of space into visually digestible areas that are not simply colorful and attractive but inviting and functional.

There is a proper preoccupation with making the market of the 90's truly a *super*market of merchandise and building design. The challenge is to make this icon of twentieth centery consumerism take it's rightful place as the anchor of the community shopping center phenomenon and hit the twenty-first century with a running start.

Adolfo R. Cruz, A.I.A., Principal
McClellan Cruz Gaylord & Associates

Chapter Five

100,000
Square Feet
And Over

Ralphs Giant

COMPTON, CA

Design: The Watt Group, Toronto, Ont., Canada

When Ralphs Grocery Co. took over several locations of approximately 100,000 sq. ft., they called upon the Watt Group to develop the model for Ralphs Giant, and to redefine the food warehouse concept for today's customers, and still feature a strong value orientation with a wide SKU base. The no-frill structures were redesigned to be places that are easy to shop and where the products are well displayed. Suspended from the metal truss ceilings are powerful 400 watt metal halide lamps which provide the primary illumination for the store.

Large red enameled space frames serve to push the graphic products murals off the perimeter walls, and they become "canopies" over wall cases and specially selected areas. Red banners are hung diagonally across the floor — from the ceiling — and tend to lower the ceiling height. Red enameled channels with fluorescent tube inserts serve to highlight some of the floor areas.

Major departmental signs are lettered in neon and float over the

main aisles so that they can readily be seen from anywhere in the operation. The neon, lower-case letters are attached to white metal grids.

The designers created a decorative look in the space through the use of metal grids and the recurring use of red. Above, in the meat area, the long run of white enameled refrigerated cases stand out in the aisles. They are banded in red. At eye level are red plaques lettered in white which specify which cuts are to be found where, and yellow signs lettered in red indicate the specials. Over the cases, in a red metal frame are fluorescent tubes behind frosted diffusers. The neon on white grid "meat" sign is visible on the right.

Jumbo Hypermarket

BUENOS AIRES, ARGENTINA

Design: International Design Group, Toronto, Ont. Canada

"Our design strategy was to create a system of fascias, signage and product photo murals that would create an overall theme. A simple and bold statement to unify the space, and at the same time help to identify the major departments" of this 100,000 sq. ft. hypermarket. It serves as an anchor for the largest shopping centre in Buenos Aires, — the Unicenter-Argentina.

The fascia that follow the perimeter of the space pop out over the traffic aisle in front of several key departments like the bakery, the deli, and the wine shop to "create an intimate and warm ambience." To further emphasize the market atmosphere, wooden carts are used in the main aisle to display special promotional items including stalls at the market. Incandescent lights are used in these areas instead of the generally "colder" fluorescents which serve to light up most of the selling space.

Promodes's Continente

VALENCIA, SPAIN

Promodes is a French mega-company that has 34,000 associates, more than $7.7 billion in consolidated wholesale and retail sales, and $10.4 billion in total business volume. Its retail business spans three types of distribution; Hypermarket, Supermarkets and neighborhood stores. The past ten years have been devoted to making Promodes Continente chain one of the largest chains of Hypermarkets in the world. For some time, most of the superstores were located in France, but the company has now expanded into Spain, Portugal and Italy. By the end of 1989, Promodes expects to have seventy Continente Hypermarkets launched.

This 108,000 sq. ft. super store is located in a high density tourist area and like the other Continente hypermarkets carries food, produce, clothes and assorted hard lines. The vast, hanger-like structure is simple and uncomplicated in design. The off-white vinyl floors reflect the light that pours down from the industrial size HID lamps that are hung from the metal trusses in the corrugated metal ceiling. The soffit over the Fresh Fish shop (Pescadero), seen on the opposite page, is a combination of wood panels with an open lattice work above it to allow the treated air to circulate through the open space. Major area signage is in neon. A rowboat and many yards of fishnet have been hung and swagged over the dark soffit in the rear of the shop. Oars, harpoons and spears are also applied as decor. Incandescent spots are set into the underside of the soffit to light up the fish on display in the cases trimmed with the same dark wood.

The Bread area (Pan), the lower picture on the opposite page, is located under a gigantic size graphic in pink and white with pink neon signage. Here too, spotlights are focused onto the fresh-made products while metal halides above light up the wide aisle. Under the soffit is an operating bakery and a service area. The photo, opposite, shows a close-up view of the cheese department which is also located beneath the very tall pink and white soffit made up of giant tiles. The cases were finished with red-orange bases.

In terms of average order, customer count, and sales per square meter, the hypermarkets now rank among the leading distribution chains in Spain.

Big Bear

AT THE MARKET OF MILL RUN, HILLIARD, OH
Design: Hixson Inc., Cincinnati, OH

With an eye towards the future, Big Bear together with Harts opened a 120,000 sq. ft. combination grocery and general merchandise store in the new Mill Run Shopping Center. The 51,000 sq. ft. Big Bear supermarket section features specialty shops located throughout the space including: a full service bakery with fresh baked goods, a delicatessen offering salads, meats, cheeses and prepared foods, a pizza shop with hand-made pizzas, a seafood shop with fresh fish from both coasts, a full service butcher shop and a special cheese section. In addition, there is a bulk food area, a walk-in beer cooler, a wine department, video rental center, soft service yogurt bar and a salad bar complete with hot soups and taco fixings.

The use of bright red starts on the

Client: Big Bear, Steve Breech, V.P.
Architect/Engineer:
Paul Frey, R.A., Project Manager, Hixson Inc.
Store Planning: Program Products and Big Bear, Inc.
Photos: Cam-Tech, Dick Loesch

outside of the brick building with the copper roof. Inside the store it is all white and red. The white vinyl tiled floors are gridded with red and bordered with black and red. Feature squares, out on the aisle, are red enameled and finished with shiny black bases. The large soffit areas are also covered with the same blazing red color. In the meat section (see previous page) a white metal space frame is suspended over the area and it carries signs in

white on red. Parts of the perimeter walls are patterned with red grids on white to stimulate giant blocks. From the metal trussed ceiling above, large HID lamps light up the selling floor below.

HVAC pipes are painted the vibrant red and become part of the decor and design of the store. Special bars or food areas are highlighted with spaceframe canopies, and some shops are given prominence on the floor by the use of illuminated red awnings. Above: One of the clothing areas in the Hart's end of this dual Hypermarket. The white aisle is also bordered in red and the selling space is carpeted in gray. In the Pharmacy, the black accents reappear in the overhead and perimeter signs, and the blue neon lettering stands out from the general lighting which is provided by the metal halide lamps recessed in the dropped ceiling.

Daimaru

KYOTO, JAPAN

Design: Chaix & Johnson, Los Angeles, CA

The two food floors of 65,000 sq. ft. each were part of the total remodeling of this noted Japanese department store in Kyoto. The design objective was to create a new store image without having to make any major structural changes.

Existing columns were used to set perimeters, — to give a definition of shape and space. "We wanted to create an image that was soft and sophisticated. Our design and style approach to this project, — with an

emphasis on light, was color and shadow."

Grayed-out pastels and soft lighting were used to create the "softness and sophistication." Since lighting was an important element in the design, tiered, lit soffit ceiling drops define the perimeters of an area — carving the space. In the produce area, metal halide lamps are combined with fluorescent luminaires. The muted teal ceramic tiled case bases are washed by fluorescents hidden beneath the white enameled cuff that wraps around the fixture. These also illuminate the white tile floors in the area.

In some of the specialty shops, the floors are paved with gray granite and separated from the white aisle by a black border. Fluorescent tubes, embedded in metal casings, form dropped "canopies" over the counters and ledges to bring the light closer to the products on display. They also provide a more gracious and intimate feeling to the space. Recessed spots in the ceiling add to the warm, soft ambience. Glass blocks are employed to enhance the contemporary look of the floor.

Hypermarket, U.S.A.

GARLAND, TX

Design: Retail Planning Associates, Columbus, OH

Two price-dominated retail formats — food and general merchandise, are incorporated into a tremendous space of 220,000 sq. ft. to become a "mall without walls" and feature Wal-Marts's "narrow but deep off-price assortment of first quality, brand name merchandise."

The interior layout includes power display aisles, large graphic banners, towers with price-value messages, a color coordinated point-of-sale system, directional kiosks and, in the food area, neon signs. The store is divided into color coded merchandise "worlds," and the floor tile colors are used to quickly establish which world the shopper has step-

ped into. The high, barrel vaulted ceilings, the arches, the exterior and front mallways are reminiscent of Grand Central Station in NYC. Glazed concrete blocks and colored metal roofing were used for economy.

The bold graphics along with the neon signs distinguish the green colored food area. Included in this world is a bakery that is capable of turning out one thousand loaves of bread an hour, a tortilla factory, a fresh and frozen sea shop and a deli. A 31,000 sq. ft. food court with a seating capacity of 219, houses non-competing food concessions. This is a mammoth enterprise.

American Fare

Located 18 miles east of Atlanta is American Fare — a truly American Hypermarket that is a joint venture of the K-Mart Corporation, — the world's second largest retailer and Bruno's, Inc. — a leading up-scaled grocery chain based in Birmingham, AL. The structure, — a one level shopping-experience, covers 244,000 sq. ft. of which 213,000 sq. ft. is used specifically for selling.

214

According to James A. Glime, the managing director of American Fare, "American Fare is designed to allow customers to shop the way they want. There is no forced 'consumer path.' Our goal is to provide a broad assortment of merchandise in a comfortable, exciting environment at prices that will bring them back."

The entire facade of the all-white building with the cool green roof serves as a large sign with heroic scaled graphics and high output lights set across the entire width of the building. The Peterson Associates designed the logo-type that would reflect the positioning of American Fare for a "new collar" audience (casual/family/focused/DYI/and active), while alluding to the merchandise categories within. Additional lifestyle characters were added across the facade as an extension of the store's identity.

During the daylight hours the mall — within — is bathed in light from the clerestorey windows. This is where the Food Court is located and to one side of it are located the leased concessions. General merchandise is available on the other side. A 20' wide, "drive aisle" down the length of the building provides easy access to the various departments — 35 different ones — that carry over 45,000 items. The departments vary from food to apparel to

hardlines, and also included are specialty shops for film processing, a card shop, a pharmacy, beauty salon, home entertainment center, florist and greenhouse.

The interior is a vast, metal and glass roofed, warehouse-style, space with well defined areas. Since there is no storage area, all the merchandise is on display, and the high-tech, black metal fixtures are on wheels

Design: Peterson Associates, Hinsdale, IL
Ted Peterson, Pres.
Dir. of Facilities Planning: Michael Fergson
Dir. Graphic Communications: Marshall S. Bohlin
Project Dir., Graphics Communications: Mick Shay
also:
Dale Wennlund, Mary Ann Einarson and
James Hanson all now with Hembrecht Terrell
International, Chicago
Apparel Fixtures: Bon Art International
Special Food Fixtures Design: P.K. Halstead
Photography:
Phots are used with the permission of
K-Mart Corp., Troy, MI

and areas can readily be repositioned as needed. The environment provides sights and smells for the shopping adventure; customers can see fish being filleted, — whiff at sausages being smoked, — smell bread being freshly baked in the largest "made from scratch" bakery, — snack on Pizzas or tacos or fried chicken. There are always flowers to delight the eye and please the senses.

To add to the happy experience, for the graphics, the signage and the decor, the designers selected a bright palette of blue-green, orange and magenta. The large fabric banners assist the shopper in locating the merchandise on the main drive aisle and in the apparel area, —

they not only add to the fun and excitement of the space, — they identify the popular national brands on display. In the Children's apparel area there are various size silhouettes on a curved wall for children to "match" themselves against — and to enable the parents to select the right size.

Lighting plays an important part in the successful designing of American Fare and it is customized to the specific areas and merchandise and yet is totally flexible. In the apparel area, an 8'x8' metal grid with track lighting attached is lowered over the merchandise to affect a more intimate scale as well as get more direct and dramatic highlighting on the merchandise.

The Deli, Seafood, and some produce "shops" are located under an overhang that stretches along the perimeter walls and the incandescent spots set into the lowered ceilings add a flattering glow to the food.

The music in the store is upbeat — in keeping with the customers in mind, and that customer is the middle to upper segment of the baby boom generation. They are educated consumers, concerned with price and value and quality. To keep them happy, with their shopping carts loaded — there are 81 checkouts to speed things up and get them out into the extensive parking lot with its 1800 spaces.

OBS!

STOCKHOLM, SWEDEN

Design: The Watts Group, Toronto, Ont., Canada

When the Swedish Cooperative Society, KF, wanted to create a new model for their OBS! Hypermarkets, they retained the Watt Group who has been innovating hypermarket designs for over 20 years. This design is a prototype for others that will be constructed in 200,000 to 250,000 sq. ft. spaces. The simple white structure would be recessive if it wasn't for the brilliant blue facade and the matching canvas awnings that make the building step forward to greet shoppers off the main highway. Even from that distance, the smart script logo — with an exclamation point — offers an invitation to a unique shopping experience.

The interior is aglow with light, — with daylight, — with HID lamps way up and some way down in milk-white frosted pendant fixtures over the arrangement of products. The color scheme appears to be basically white and black with red and green used to add some excitement. Below, in produce, white vinyl floors are complemented by white ceramic tiled floors. Insert strips of black and white ceramic tiles in a checkerboard design serve as borders, dividers and directionals on the floor. To bring the large open space more into scale with the shoppers, a giant green metal canopy stretches over the matching green tubular fixtures on the floor. The pendants hang from this super structure as do graphics and signage. The green signs with white lettering blend with the fixtures, unify the design and are still readily seen and easily read. Opposite this area, on the right, is the Delikatessen. A soffit sign of yellow and red neon identifies the shop which is located beneath a lowered ceiling. A red ceiling grid, red tiles accenting the white rear wall and white refrigerated cases banded in red create a bright, effective change from the emphasis on green outside.

Fashion accessories and costume jewelry are sold in an even more "intimate" setting. A white grid is lowered to about 10' off the ground and it carries a plentiful arrange-

ment of fluorescent strip lighting.
Pyramid shaped lighting elements
are fitted over counters and free
standing fixtures to provide warm,
flattering light at the points of sale.
The selling space, off the white tile
aisle is accented with a deep green
and terra cotta colored floor, and
all the fixtures and frames are
white. Neon signage identifies the
department.

The softwear and fashion areas of

the hypermarket are treated more like areas in a department or specialty shop. The real ceiling has been painted out with a dark, disappearing color and a wood grid canopy, painted light green, is hung at a comfortable and "intimate height" of 10' off the green tiled floor. White slatwall partitions separate the various divisions of the fashion area, and they carry merchandise as well as front-on merchandise displays. Rows of track lights are attached to the ceiling grid and they supply warm incandescent light to the garments on the floor and the walls. The Hypermarket also has a complete service cafe/restaurant ready to accommodate the hungry hoards who come to spend a profitable day of shopping at OBS!

Carrefour, U.S.A.

BUCKS COUNTY, PA

Design: Rafael Vincoly Architects, NY

Europe and South America, into the U.S. market, — and this is their largest hypermarket to date. The operation combines a supermarket with apparel, consumer electronics, automotive, soft goods and hardware departments along with specialty tenant stores.

The entire facade is constructed of a horizontally striped metal panel system. Brightly colored stucco arcades and a glass and aluminum entry pavilion reflect the contemporary merchandising philosophy of the client.

The structure utilizes a pre-engineered building system which has been architecturally reinterpreted. The composition of large scale elements, plus the arcades and entry pavilion tend to reduce the apparent size of the building to provide a more up-scale shopping

This mammoth 330,000 sq. ft., one story, structure sits on a 37-acre site and is surrounded by 2,000 parking spaces. It represents the entrance of the well known French retail chain, with over 100 stores throughout

center image. There are several very wide aisles that intersect through the space, and the area is largely illuminated by metal halide lamps. Fluorescents and incandescents also appear in some of the specialized shops that hug the perimeter walls. Neon signs, on the soffits — over the specialty shops, add some color to the otherwise, light neutral space. Working bakeries, butcher shops and fish shops add to the theater of the hypermarket. Carrefour represents a "new way to shop," and they describe their layout as "logical and (we) use common sense to make your shopping experience easier and faster." How fast can it go when the service help whips around on skates and skate boards?

Index of Design Articles